A New Library of the Supernatural
the Supernatural

Index to Occult Sciences

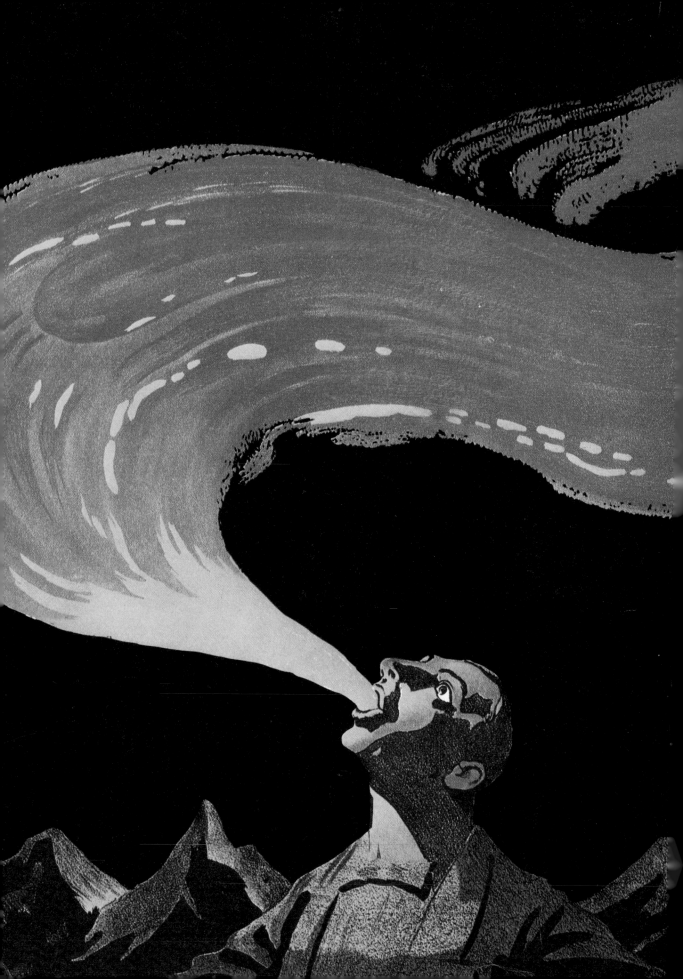

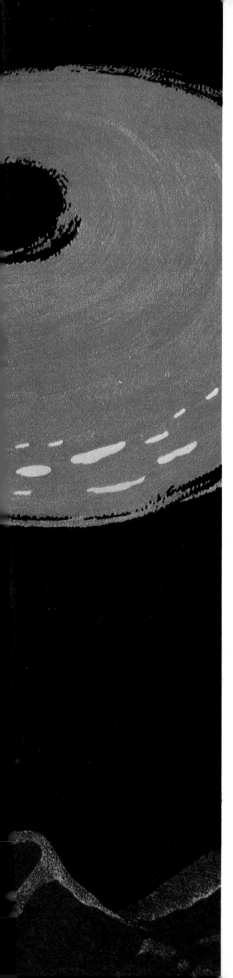

Index to Occult Sciences

Also published as Guide and Index

Doubleday and Company, Inc.
Garden City, New York, 1977

EDITORIAL CONSULTANTS:

COLIN WILSON
DR. CHRISTOPHER EVANS

Series Coordinator: John Mason
Design Director: Günter Radtke
Picture Editor: Peter Cook
Designer: Ann Dunn
Editor: Sally Burningham
Copy Editor: Mitzi Bales
Research: Frances Vargo
General Consultant: Beppie Harrison

Library of Congress Cataloging in Publication Data
Main entry under title:
Index to Occult Sciences

(A New Library of the Supernatural)

1. Occult sciences—Biography   2. Psychical
research—Biography   3. A New Library of
the Supernatural—Indexes
BF1408.15   133'.092'2   [B]   76–40569
1SBN 0-385-11326-9

Doubleday and Company
ISBN: 0-385-11326-9
Library of Congress Catalog
Card No. 76-40569
A New Library of the Supernatural
ISBN: 11327-7
© Aldus Books Limited, London
D. L. S.S.: 317/76
Printed and bound in Spain
by TONSA San Sebastián
and RONER Madrid

**Frontispiece: magician or mystic? Shaman or sham?
Above: a stage illusionist conjures up a spirit.**

Index to Occult Sciences

Men and women with psychic gifts have been with us since the earliest times, and the accounts of the unexplained phenomena they produce continue to fascinate people today. The biographical sketches in this book are a kind of index to leading occult figures and their investigators, past and present.

Contents

ABRAMS, DR. ALBERT (1863–1924)

Director of the Medical Department of Stanford University and pioneer of radionics. Born into a wealthy San Francisco family, Abrams qualified as a doctor in Heidelberg, Germany, and carried out postgraduate studies in London, Vienna, and Berlin. He returned to San Francisco and became quickly established as an eminent neurologist with an international reputation. His interest was absorbed by the discovery that patients suffering various diseases emitted electromagnetic vibrations of a different intensity from each other and from those of healthy people. He invented a machine known as a reflexophone to measure these vibrations and diagnose disease. He also came to believe that diseases could be broken down and cured by the application of measured vibrations. To do so he constructed an oscilloclast, known as the Black Box. Although great interest was aroused by Abrams' experiments, his ideas were not accepted by orthodox medicine, and he died a disappointed man.

ADAMS, EVANGELINE (1865–1932)

Famous American astrologer who popularized astrology in the United States. In 1899 Evangeline Adams moved from her hometown of Boston to New York and created an immediate sensation. She told the proprietor of the Windsor Hotel, where she was staying, that he was "under one of the worst possible combinations of planets." Next day the hotel burned down, killing the proprietor's daughter and several members of his family. He told the story to the press, and Evangeline Adams' reputation as a forecaster was established. She opened a studio above Carnegie Hall, and her clients soon included famous movie stars, politicians, and financiers. In 1914 she was prosecuted for fortune telling, but the judge was so impressed by the accuracy of her reading from the birth date of a person unknown to her that he dismissed the case against her. In 1930 she started a radio program on astrology, through which she received thousands of requests from listeners each day. In 1931 she prophesied that the United States would be at war in 1942. In 1932 she forecast her own death that year, and when she died in November thousands of clients and fans came to see her body lying in state at Carnegie Hall. Evangeline Adams' books include: *Astrology: Your Place Among the Stars*, which became a best-seller, and *Astrology: Your Place in the Sun*.

ADAMSKI, GEORGE (1891–1965)

Polish-born American who claimed he met visitors from Venus, Mars, and Saturn, and that they traveled to earth in flying saucers. Adamski worked as a handyman in a café near the Mount Palomar Hale Observatory in California. From an early age he believed that other planets were inhabited, and in 1946 he claimed to have seen a gigantic UFO hovering above the mountain ridge to the south of Mount Palomar. In 1952 Adamski made his first contact with visitors from outer space. With six companions he drove into the California desert and communicated by telepathy and sign language with a human-looking Venusian who stepped out of a flying saucer. Adamski's six friends confirmed seeing the encounter from a distance. Later

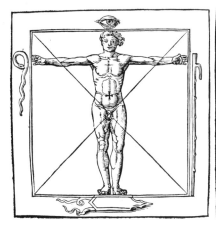
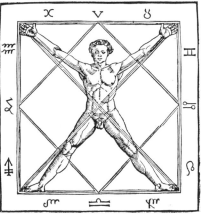

he claimed he met space dwellers who looked like ordinary people in a Los Angeles hotel, and they took him for a ride in their flying saucer. Adamski wrote *Flying Saucers Have Landed* in 1953 with British author Desmond Leslie, and *Inside the Space Ships* in 1956.

AGRIPPA, CORNELIUS (1486–1535)

German scholar with an interest in magic. He wrote *The Occult Philosophy*, which is still considered one of the greatest books on magic. Agrippa, whose real name was Heinrich Cornelius, was born in Cologne, and at the age of 20 became court secretary to the Holy Roman Emperor. But he was more interested in philosophy and magic than in politics, and began to study the Cabala, a Jewish system of mystical knowledge. Agrippa was often in violent conflict with the clergy, and was driven out of many towns after clashes with the local priests. He was accused of black magic, and many legends grew up about him. The impression is given in *The Occult Philosophy* that Agrippa had gifts of clairvoyance and telepathy, and the ability to influence events by the power of his mind. He studied alchemy for many years, but was finally disillusioned.

ARIGÓ, JOSÉ (1918–71)

Brazilian psychic surgeon. Arigó, whose real name was José Pedro de Freitas, was born in Congonhas do Campo. As a boy he had mystical experiences, seeing mysterious moving lights and hearing voices speaking to him in strange languages. In the 1950s Arigó came under the influence of a spirit control known as "Dr. Fritz," a German surgeon killed in World War I. He began to perform hundreds of successful operations, working without anesthetics and using unsterilized instruments such as kitchen knives, nail scissors, and tweezers. A group of South American doctors witnessed an operation in which Arigó removed a tumor from a young woman's womb, using ordinary scissors. The woman remained conscious throughout the operation, and apparently felt no pain. Arigó sealed the cut simply by pressing the edges together. Arigó did his operations in a trance state. Once when he saw a photograph of one of them, he got sick. In 1964 Arigó was charged under a law making spiritual healing a crime, and was sent to prison for 16 months. After his release, he did not perform any more psychic operations.

B

BAKER, GEORGE "Father Divine" (1880–1965)

American black cult figure. Born on a rice plantation in South Carolina, George Baker first came to public notice when he founded religious communities that he called "heavens." His disciples were known as "angels," and they took vows of temperance and chastity, giving up all worldly goods and devoting their services free to the cult. Later George Baker moved to Long Island, and in 1930 was reborn as "Father Divine." He had great charisma, and won many followers when he became a champion of unemployed blacks during the Depression. By 1936 Father Divine had 160 Peace Missions in the United States, among which were some white members. Among his followers sexual relations, even between husband and wife, were considered sinful, and alcohol and tobacco were banned. He married twice, but claimed that his marriages were purely spiritual. However, he always surrounded himself with beautiful women. Father Divine had a large number of businesses including barber shops, laundries, restaurants, and garages. He was fond of wearing silk suits and jeweled rings, and had a fleet of cars including one of 265-horsepower that became famous as the Throne Car. It was estimated that Father Divine was worth about $10 million when he died.

BENDER, DR. HANS (b. 1907)

German psychologist and researcher in parapsychology. Dr. Bender was born in Freiburg, Germany, the son of a lawyer. He studied and lectured in psychology at various European universities before becoming Professor for the Border Areas of Psychology at Freiburg University in 1954. He edited the *Journal of Parapsychology and Border Areas of Psychology*, and has written *New Developments in Poltergeist Research* and other works about parapsychology, dream psychology, and the psychology

Below: Father Divine, American cult figure of the 20th century, walks in front of his bride-to-be on their wedding day in 1946. In line with his edict against all sexual relationships, Father Divine claimed that his two marriages were of a spiritual nature.

of superstition. One of his most interesting investigations was of Anne-Marie, a German girl who seemingly and unconsciously caused electrical explosions, the movement of heavy objects, and disturbances in the telephone equipment in her place of employment. Bender concluded that Anne-Marie's dislike of the office expressed itself in poltergeist activity. After studying the case of the Nickelheim family, in whose house stones and other objects seemed to move in and out of closed rooms, Dr. Bender said science may have to consider the existence of "higher space," which would allow "four-fold freedom of movement" and the penetration of matter by matter. Dr. Bender has also investigated voice phenomena on tape recordings, and suggests that electronic impulses are sent out by the subconscious mind and register as human speech on the tape. Dr. Bender is one of the few academics to carry out scientific research in astrology. After World War II he tested more than 100 astrologers, using "blind diagnosis," in which astrologers were given anonymous horoscopes to read.

BENNETT, ALLAN (1872–1923)

British electrical engineer who became a Buddhist monk after being introduced to mysticism through the Golden Dawn and the Theosophical Society. While a member of the Golden Dawn, Bennett wrote and took part in a magical ceremony called "Ritual for the Evocation unto Visible Appearance of the Great Spirit Taphthartharath," in which the spirit is said to have materialized. There is evidence that one, if not all, of the participants had taken drugs to heighten or induce the experience. In 1900 Bennett went to Ceylon to study Buddhism and became a monk, taking the name of Ananda Metteya. One story has it that when Bennett was at a monastery in Burma, he was seen hovering weightless in the air, blown about like a leaf. Bennett had a big influence on the British Buddhist Society, which was founded in 1908.

BERLITZ, CHARLES (b. 1914)

American archeologist, underwater explorer, and author, who became convinced that mysterious powers destroy boats and planes in what he calls "The Bermuda Triangle." Berlitz was born in New York City and educated at Yale University. He is a member of the family that founded the Berlitz School of Languages, and has linguistic skill himself, having written over 200 books on the teaching of languages. Other of his books are on prehistoric archeology and underwater research. In *The Mystery of Atlantis,* a book written with Dr. Manson Valentine, an American archeologist and oceanographer, Berlitz claims that an entire city lies submerged off the coast of Haiti, and that there is an underwater road off north Bimini in the Bahamas. He also writes that the Soviets have found an underwater building complex covering over 10 acres of sea floor north of Cuba. His book *The Bermuda Triangle* gives cases of ships and planes that have disappeared in a triangular area within the Atlantic Ocean, and investigates reports of people who narrowly escaped. Berlitz's other recent books include *Mysteries from Forgotten Worlds* and *Dive.*

Below: Charles Berlitz, author of many language instruction books as well as the controversial *Bermuda Triangle,* shown editing one of his books. Perhaps because of his interest in the sea, he works on a moored cargo ship in what was the captain's cabin.

Above: Rosemary Brown, British medium who produces music said to be the work of dead great masters. *Rosemary Brown's Music*, a disk of compositions dictated to her from the spirit world, was issued in 1970. Rosemary Brown is also a Spiritualist and faith healer.

BLAVATSKY, MADAME ELENA PETROVNA (1831–91)

One of the founders of the Theosophical Society, through which she played a leading role in the revival of occultism in Europe and the United States in the late 19th century. Different members of the Society were interested in different aspects of occultism— for example, study of the Cabala, Spiritualism, and ancient and eastern religions. Later the Theosophists put more emphasis on the formation of "the nucleus of a universal brotherhood of humanity," and their doctrines became popular in progressive circles in the West. Madame Blavatsky was born in Russia, the daughter of Colonel Peter Hahn. She married at 16 but left her husband soon after. She then traveled the world, often in the company of male companions, and at one time worked as a bareback rider in a circus. Madame Blavatsky was a theatrical, flamboyant woman with great magnetic appeal. Odd things continually happened in her presence, such as inexplicable rappings, ringing of bells, and movement of objects. In 1873 she arrived penniless in the United States. She met an American lawyer, Colonel H. S. Olcott, who was a keen psychic investigator, and together they began to study Spiritualism. She convinced him that she was in touch with priests of ancient Egypt. They held meetings for like-minded people and in 1875 founded the Theosophical Society. In 1879 they moved the headquarters of the Society to India, where Madame Blavatsky was an immediate success. She persuaded her followers that she was guided by the Secret Masters of Tibet, who were godlike creatures. When disciples asked questions, paper notes signed by "Koot Hoomi," one of the Secret Masters, fell from the air. Then scandal broke. Letters were published which seemed to indicate that Madame Blavatsky's manifestations were due to trickery. The Society of Psychical Research in London sent their expert, Richard Hodgson, to investigate, and he declared Madame Blavatsky to be a fraud. She retired to Europe, but the work of the Theosophical Society continued to flourish under the leadership of Mrs. Annie Besant and others. Madame Blavatsky wrote several books, including *Isis Unveiled* (1877) and *The Secret Doctrine* (1888), which she said were inspired by the Secret Masters.

BROWN, ROSEMARY (b. about 1917)

British automatic writer who, since 1964, has been writing music that she claims is dictated by the great composers of the past. According to Mrs. Brown, she has been seeing and talking to spirits from early youth, the composer Liszt first appearing to her when she was seven years old. In 1964 Mrs. Brown had an accident; shortly afterward Liszt appeared and began dictating music to her. Later Liszt introduced Chopin, Beethoven, Brahms, Bach, Debussy, Grieg, Rachmaninov, and Stravinsky to Mrs. Brown who took down their compositions as they dictated them. Many famous musicians have been impressed with the compositions. Others say that, though they are in the style of the great masters, they are not of the quality of their best compositions. Rosemary Brown is a Spiritualist who also practices faith healing. A record called *Rosemary Brown's Music* was issued in 1970.

C

Right: the Italian known as Count Cagliostro. A bold adventurer, he became rich and famous for his healing and other occult powers in most of 18th-century Europe. However, he died in poverty.

Below: this illustration shows Cagliostro trying to convince a group of Latvian nobles that the nine-year-old boy he has in tow is a medium. According to report, his attempt did not succeed.

CAGLIOSTRO, COUNT ALESSANDRO DI
(1743–about 1795)

Italian adventurer with apparent occult powers, whose real name was probably Giuseppe Balsamo. Born of peasant stock in Palermo, Sicily, he became a wanderer in his teens, living on his wits and studying alchemy, astrology, and ritual magic. In 1769 he married Lorenza, the beautiful 14-year-old daughter of a coppersmith, who became his partner in fraud. They visited England where Cagliostro joined the Freemasons. He then founded his own masonic order and traveled about Europe introducing magic rituals which he claimed to have discovered in an ancient Egyptian manuscript. He also became famous for his healing powers. He seems to have been an odd mixture of charlatan and philanthropist. In 1785 he became involved in a scandal over a diamond necklace in France. He was tried and acquitted, but the months he spent in the Bastille before the trial broke his nerve and ruined his reputation. He was hounded by the police for the rest of his life, and finally died in the prison fortress of San Leone in Urbino, Italy.

CARRINGTON, DR. HEREWARD (1881–1959)

Distinguished English psychic researcher and author of many books on psychic subjects. Dr. Carrington joined the British Society of Psychical Research at the age of 19 and devoted the rest of his life to psychic studies. He investigated the Italian medium Eusapia Paladino in Naples, and wrote *Eusapia Paladino and her Phenomena*. In *Personal Experiences in Spiritualism* (1918) he speculated that spiritualist phenomena are essentially of biological origin. He attended many seances with Mrs. Leonore Piper, the American trance medium, and subjected the medium Mrs. Eileen Garrett to psychoanalytical tests at the American Psychical Institute which he founded in 1921. His studies of Mrs. Garrett convinced him of "the existence of mental entities independent of the control of the medium, and separate and apart from the conscious or subconscious mind of the medium." After writing *Modern Psychical Phenomena*, which included a chapter on astral projection, Dr. Carrington became acquainted with Sylvan Muldoon, the famous American "astral traveler." Together they wrote *The Projection of the Astral Body* (1929).

CASTANEDA, DR. CARLOS (b. 1931)

American anthropologist who became an apprentice to a Yaqui Indian sorcerer, and wrote several books about his psychic experiences. Castaneda was born in São Paulo, Brazil, and graduated from the University of California. He now lives in Los Angeles. In 1961, while visiting the southwest to study the medicinal plants used by the Indians, he met Don Juan, a Yaqui Indian from Sonora, Mexico. Don Juan was held in great awe because of his strange powers. He adopted Castaneda as his apprentice, introduced the anthropologist to substances that alter perception, and taught him astral projection. Castaneda claims that he once turned into a crow, and flew with perfect confidence at the sorcerer's command. Castaneda is the author of: *The Teachings of Don Juan: a Yaqui Way of Knowledge* (1968); *Journey to Ixtlan: The Last Lessons of Don Juan; A Separate Reality* (1971); and *Tales of Power* (1974). Some people claim that Castaneda's books are works of fiction rather than anthropological studies.

CAYCE, EDGAR (1877–1945)

American healer and clairvoyant known as "The Sleeping Prophet." Cayce (pronounced "Casey") was born on a Kentucky farm, and left school after the sixth grade. A slim, stoop-shouldered man with a kindly gaze, he was very religious and read the Bible every day. Although he had no medical knowledge whatsoever he found that in a trance state he was able to diagnose his own illness and suggest a possible cure. He then went on to diagnose other people's sickness and to prescribe effective treatments. It was usually unnecessary for him to meet the patient or know anything about the illness. All he needed was a name and address. He claimed to have treated about 30,000 people, and records of his trance readings are kept at the Association for Research and Enlightenment (ARE) in Virginia Beach. It is claimed that on many occasions Cayce prescribed

Below: Dr. Carlos Casteneda, an anthropologist who experimented with sorcery, avoids having his picture taken so that people will not recognize him and ask about his strange psychic experiences.

medicines that were not yet generally available, and often suggested remedies that had long been forgotten, but when checked by pharmacists were found to be effective. Until 1923 Cayce gave medical advice only, but from that date he began tracing people's past lives while in trance. He also made numerous references to Atlantis while in deep trance. He believed that some of the contacts in his "psychic interviews" were former inhabitants of Atlantis which, he claimed, was a technically advanced civilization that may have been destroyed by nuclear power. He believed that beneath the Egyptian pyramids lie secret libraries of knowledge from the lost continent of Atlantis. According to his sons, Edgar Cayce had not read Plato's material or any books on Atlantis. Supporters claim that Cayce predicted the Wall Street Crash of 1929; the hurricanes, earthquakes, and tidal waves that hit California, Japan, and the Philippines in 1926; the discovery of the Dead Sea Scrolls; and the invention of laser beams. Like several other prophets, he predicted a cataclysmic war about 2000, and the end of civilization as we know it shortly after.

Above: Edgar Cayce, an American psychic who diagnosed illnesses in trance, shown in court with his wife and secretary after being charged with telling fortunes. His case was dismissed by a New York magistrate on a technicality.

CHEIRO (1866–1936)
Famous palmist and writer of many books on palmistry and other methods of fortune telling. Cheiro, whose real name was Count Louis Hamon, was born in Ireland. He took his pseu-

Right: this model of a palm shows the names of the lines and areas to be read in character analysis.

Below: Cheiro, a modern palmist, wrote many textbooks on palmistry. He had a reputation for making many predictions that came true.

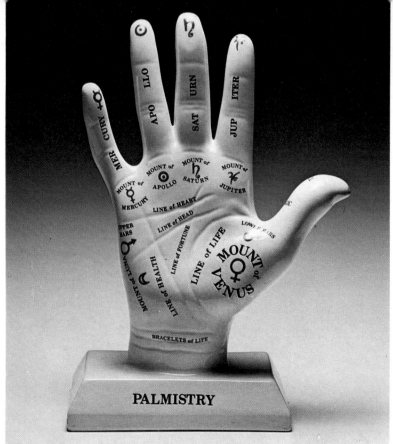

PALMISTRY

donym from the Greek word *cheir* meaning hand. Cheiro had extensive knowledge of both chirognomy, which is the telling of character from the hands, and chiromancy, which is reading the future in the hands. His clients included many famous people. Some unusual predictions made by Cheiro are known to have come true. One of the most famous is the prophecy he made in 1894 for Lord Kitchener, a leading British general then 44 years old. He foretold that in 1916 Kitchener would meet with disaster at sea unless he could avoid traveling on the water in that year. Kitchener ignored the warning. He died at sea in 1916 on the cruiser *H.M.S. Hampshire*, which struck a German mine off the north coast of Scotland.

CHURCHWARD, COLONEL JAMES (b. mid-19th century) English army officer who claimed to have discovered the ancient civilization of Mu. While serving in India in 1868, Colonel Churchward met a Hindu priest, from whom he learned an ancient language called Naacal. This was believed to be the original tongue of mankind. Using his knowledge of Naacal, Churchward deciphered a number of ancient stone tablets of which the Hindu priest was the custodian. These tablets revealed the existence of Mu, a large continent that, before sinking beneath the Pacific Ocean, had been the Garden of Eden. Churchward also deciphered thousands of stone objects found in Mexico by an American engineer, William Niven. He said that the Niven tablets were at least 12,000 years old and that, like the Naacal tablets, they were extracts from the Sacred Inspired Writings of Mu. Churchward claimed that Mu had a highly sophisticated culture, and before the continent was destroyed by volcanoes, the population totaled 64 million. All human races developed from Mu. The most powerful of Mu's colonies was the Uighur Empire, now buried beneath the Gobi Desert, but the Uighur survivors became the Aryans. An essential feature of Churchward's theory was that the colored tribes of Mu were subservient to the white tribes. His books are: *The Lost Continent of Mu* (1926), *The Children of Mu* (1931), *The Sacred Symbols of Mu* (1933), and *Cosmic Forces of Mu* (1934).

CONDON, DR. EDWARD U. (b. 1902)
American physicist who directed a scientific study of flying saucers for the United States Air Force between 1966 and 1968. Dr. Condon was born in Alamogordo, New Mexico, and taught physics at Columbia and Princeton Universities. The United States Air Force allocated $500,000 to Condon's UFO committee. When the Condon Report was published in 1969 it said that nothing of value to science had come from the study of UFO sightings, and that further investigation was pointless. It was widely believed in American UFO circles that Dr. Condon was party to a coverup, based on political considerations.

COOK, FLORENCE (1856–1904)
English trance medium whose claim to have produced the materialization of a complete human form aroused a storm of controversy. From an early age Florence Cook had practiced table-turning, levitation, and automatic writing. While still very young, she began to hold seances. After she sat in a dark curtained recess for a time, a spirit form would emerge. The spirit, known as Katie King, was dressed in white. Though she looked like Florence herself there were certain physical differences, and the whole question hinged on whether they could be one and the same person. Sir William Crookes, the famous scientist who became a psychic investigator in late life, observed Florence Cook over a long period and believed that Katie King was a genuine materialization. However, the tests that he carried out with her were less scientific than those he had conducted in his other work, although he claimed to have taken a photograph of Florence Cook and Katie King together.

CROISET, GERARD (b. 1909)
Dutch psychometrist, who often uses his power to read an object's history by touching it in the service of the police. Croiset was an unhealthy child and spent much of his childhood in foster homes. From an early age he was clairvoyant, able to describe things happening in other places. At the age of 25 he picked up a stick in a friend's house, and immediately had an image of a car accident and a body lying by the roadside. From then on he practiced psychometry. When working for the police, Croiset is given objects found at the scene of a crime. He can often describe the incident and the criminal in enough detail to contribute to the solution of the case.

CROOKALL, DR. ROBERT (b. 1890)
Leading British researcher on astral projection. He lectured in botany at Aberdeen University in Scotland and then for many

Above: Gerard Croiset has the psychic gift of being able to tell things about an object and its owner simply by touching it. He often uses his powers to help the police in investigations of crime.

years was principal geologist at the government's Geological Survey in London. Since his retirement in 1952 he has devoted his life to studying out-of-the-body experiences (OOBEs). Dr. Crookall has collected thousands of reports of OOBEs from all over the world. He believes that during astral projection the "vital body" and the "soul body," the center of thinking, leave the physical body. He says that in the first stage of astral projection the vital body is connected to the physical body by a silvery cord. After a person has died, he claims, many observers have seen the vital body as a vaporous substance emerging from the head. It remains linked to the physical body for three days and then disappears. The body that lasts for eternity he calls the "spirit body." Dr. Crookall is the author of *The Study and Practice of Astral Projection* (1961); *The Techniques of Astral Projection* (1964); *Case-book of Astral Projection* (1972); *The Interpretation of Cosmic and Mystical Experiences* (1969); *Intimations of Immortality* (1965); *During Sleep* (1974), and *Ecstasy* (1974).

CROOKES, SIR WILLIAM (1832–1919)
Eminent British scientist and president of the Society for Psychical Research. As a scientist he made many important discoveries including the metal thallium. He invented the radiometer, founded *Chemical News*, and edited the *Quarterly Journal of Science*. Awarded many academic honors, he was at different times president of the Chemical Society, the Institution of Elcctrical Engineers, and the Royal Society. He was also keenly interested in Spiritualism and investigated many mediums. From 1896–9 he was president of the Society for Psychical Research. Crookes used specially designed apparatus to test the medium Daniel Dunglas Home. Crookes believed that these tests conclusively proved the existence of a new force that for convenience he termed the Psychic Force. The Royal Society refused to publish his findings. Crookes also reported favorably

Above: Sir William Crookes was the foremost authority on industrial chemistry in his day, and invented several pieces of apparatus for use in chemistry and physics. He was among the first scientists to make a serious study of psychic phenomena, especially as related to Spiritualism.

Right: the flamboyant magician and cult figure Aleister Crowley in an unusually relaxed pose.

on other mediums, but his investigation of Florence Cook was conducted far less scientifically, it was claimed, and gave rise to much hostile criticism.

CROWLEY, ALEISTER (1875–1947)

Student of the occult, alleged magician, and cult figure. Crowley was born in Leamington, Warwickshire. His father was a brewer and belonged to a very strict Christian sect, the Plymouth Brethren. He soon rebelled against his Christian family background, and his mother believed him to be the Beast 666 of the Apocalypse, an identity which Crowley was pleased to claim throughout his life. While still at university in Cambridge he became interested in magic, and joined the Golden Dawn. In his twenties Crowley began taking drugs, went mountaineering in the Himalayas, published several volumes of poetry, and traveled in Mexico, Hawaii, Ceylon, and India. In India he studied yoga, Buddhism, and the sexual techniques of Tantra. Crowley believed himself to be a reincarnation of Pope Alexander VI, the Egyptian priest Ankh-f-n-Khonsu, Eliphas Lévi, Cagliostro, and others. In 1903 while on honeymoon in Cairo, Crowley received messages through the medium of his bride, Rose Kelly. They were supposed to be from Aiwass, one of the Secret Chiefs whom Crowley said ruled the universe. These messages were incorporated in *The Book of the Law*, which Crowley wrote and which contains his basic philosophy: "Do what thou wilt shall be the whole of the law." After the collapse of the Golden Dawn, Crowley developed his own Order of the Silver Star. He also became head of the British branch of the Ordo Templis Orientis, a society founded in Germany in 1902 and devoted to the teaching of sexual magic. In 1920 he founded his Abbey of Thelema in Sicily. Crowley believed that mankind was moving into a new age, of which he was the prophet. Expelled from Sicily in 1923, he died in obscurity in Hastings, England.

Below: *The Island of Magicians,* a watercolor by Crowley done in 1921. At that time he was living in Sicily as the master of his Abbey of Thelema, devoted to sexual magic and other occult study.

Right: a rare lithograph of the Davenport brothers in 1864. Ira and William produced phenomena on stage together for some years.

Below: the Davenports at a "dark seance," so called because it was conducted in total darkness. One candle and matches were kept on hand for lighting when needed.

DAVENPORT brothers, IRA ERASTUS (1838–1911) and
WILLIAM HENRY (1841–77)
American mediums who gave demonstrations on stage before
large audiences. Ira and William were the sons of a Buffalo police
officer. From about the year 1846 mysterious bumps and loud
noises began to occur in their house, and in 1850 the boys and
their younger sister Elisabeth decided to try their hand at table-
turning. Raps were heard, messages were spelled out, Ira's
hand was seized to write automatically, and it is claimed that
on one occasion the three children levitated simultaneously.
During their later theater performances, Ira and William were
tied immobile inside a special cabinet that audiences were
invited to inspect. Within seconds of the doors of the cabinet
being closed, the immobilized brothers would nonetheless produce raps, musical sounds, and other phenomena. They became
particularly famous for their ability to release themselves from
complicated knots. Ira and William never presented themselves
as Spiritualists, although their phenomena resembled those at
spiritualist seances. Houdini, the world-famous escape artist,
claimed that he could produce all their effects by trickery. On a
visit to England in 1864 the Davenport brothers met hostile
audiences although they were never proved to be frauds.

DEE, DR. JOHN (1527–1608)
Elizabethan scholar, mathematician, astrologer, and alchemist.
Dee was born of Welsh parents, the son of an official at the
court of King Henry VIII. He went to Cambridge University at
the age of 15, and became a fellow of Trinity College only four
years later. He traveled and studied abroad, meeting the Flemish
cartographer Mercator in 1547. He took two of Mercator's
globes back to England as well as knowledge of new astronomical
instruments and navigational methods that were to prove invalu-
able. Having read Agrippa's *Occult Philosophy*, he became increasingly interested in magic, especially in the areas which at
that time seemed to border on science. He cast horoscopes both
for the reigning Queen Mary and for her sister Elizabeth. Mary,
suspicious of his relationship with Elizabeth and thinking that
he might be plotting with her, flung him into prison where he
remained until 1555. After his release he lived in seclusion until
Elizabeth came to the throne in 1558. Elizabeth regularly con-
sulted Dee on astrology and sent him abroad again, probably as
a spy. In spite of the queen's friendship Dee was regarded with
suspicion by many because of his interest in crystal gazing and
magic.

DEMENT, DR. WILLIAM CHARLES (b. 1928)
Psychiatrist and dream researcher. Dr. Dement was born in
Wenatchee, Washington, and qualified as a doctor at the University of Chicago. In 1960 he began a series of dream experiments at Mount Sinai Hospital, New York City. In 1963 he
became Director of the Sleep Laboratory at Stanford University
Medical School, and since 1970 has been Director of the Sleep
Disorders Clinic at Stanford. Dr. Dement and his colleagues
found that dream deprivation makes people tired, irritable, and
subject to memory loss in the morning. They decided that dreams

are essential to psychological and physical health. They found a direct correspondence between a sleeper's eye movements and the images in his dreams. For example, a person who dreamed about climbing stairs showed vertical movements of the eyes. Sensory stimuli, such as a spray of water, was found to influence the images in a dream, but Dr. Dement concluded that although external stimuli may be incorporated into a dream, the sleeper plots his own scenario and decides the theme.

DIXON, JEANE (b. 1918)

America's most famous living clairvoyant. When Jeane was eight years old and living in California, a gipsy fortune teller said: "This little girl is going to be world famous. . . . she is blessed with a gift for prophecy. Never have I seen such palm lines." Later Jeane Dixon discovered that she had extrasensory powers far greater than other people's. Tests showed that her ESP ability was 90 to 97 percent compared with 3 to 7 percent for the average person. Jeane Dixon, who is a deeply religious woman, learned astrology from a Jesuit priest in Los Angeles, and though she prefers to use a crystal for personal readings, she believes it is also possible to read the stars. She makes a distinction between God-given revelations about future events which cannot be changed, and premonitions of possible future dangers which she receives through telepathy, and which can be avoided. "Jeane Dixon's Horoscope" column appears in hundreds of American papers, and her predictions are closely followed. She foretold the deaths of astronauts Grissom, White, and Chaffee in the fire that destroyed Apollo 4 in January 1967, and she forecast the deaths of UN Secretary Dag Hammarskjold and Mahatma Gandhi. Her most dramatic predictions concerned the political murders in the United States in the 1960s. In 1952, it is said, Jeane Dixon had a vision of a young blue-eyed man with a shock of brown hair who would be elected president in 1960, and would be assassinated while in office. John Kennedy was elected president in 1960 and was murdered in 1963; his funeral mass was said in the very church where Jeane Dixon had her vision. In 1968, it is said, she told a group of people that Martin Luther King would be shot and "Robert Kennedy will be next." A few days later King was assassinated. Jeane Dixon repeated her warning about Robert Kennedy at a convention in the Ambassador Hotel, Los Angeles, on May 28th, 1968, and on June 5 the senator was murdered in the same hotel.

Above: Jeane Dixon, the most famous psychic in the United States. She generally uses a crystal to foresee the future, but is also well-known for reading the stars.

DONNELLY, IGNATIUS T. T. (1831–1901)

American lawyer and congressman who stimulated interest in the ancient legends of Atlantis with his book *Atlantis, the Antediluvian World*, published in 1882. Donnelly was born in Philadelphia, where he studied law and was admitted to the bar at the age of 22. In 1856 he and some friends bought land near St. Paul, Minnesota, where they hoped to build a great Middlewest Metropolis, Nininger City. The plan never materialized and Donnelly turned to politics, becoming Lieutenant-Governor of Minnesota in 1859, and a member of the United States congress from 1863 to 1870. When his wife died he spent long hours in the Library of Congress, and began writing. *Atlantis, the Ante-*

Above: Mexican pottery said by Ignatius T. T. Donnelly, influential writer on the lost continent of Atlantis, to be models of Atlanteans. He believed that some survivors of Atlantis had settled in Mexico. Left: Sir Arthur Conan Doyle in Egypt. His interest in the occult took the famous creator of Sherlock Holmes to faraway places.

diluvian World created a great sensation, and has been reprinted at least 50 times. Donnelly followed this with *Ragnarok: the Age of Fire and Gravel* (1883), which describes natural cataclysms such as the one that allegedly submerged Atlantis; and *The Great Cryptogram* (1888) in which he sought to prove that Bacon wrote Shakespeare's works. Donnelly believed that Atlantis was a huge continent in the Atlantic ocean where civilization was first attained. It was destroyed about 13,000 years ago, but a few inhabitants escaped and fled to the Gulf of Mexico, the Amazon, the Mediterranean, the west coasts of Africa and Europe, and other regions. Donnelly claimed that the Phoenician alphabet, the origin of all European alphabets, was a form of the Atlantis alphabet, and that gods and goddesses of Greek, Phoenician, and Scandinavian mythology were a folk memory of the kings and queens of Atlantis. Donnelly argued that the resemblance between many species of American and European plants, and the existence of pyramids on both sides of the Atlantic were due to a common origin in Atlantis. His books have influenced many later writers on Atlantis.

DOYLE, SIR ARTHUR CONAN (1858–1930)
Creator of the Sherlock Holmes detective stories, and a Spiritu-

alist. Conan Doyle was born in Edinburgh, Scotland, the son of an Irish Catholic family. He qualified as a doctor at Edinburgh University and practiced medicine in Southsea, Hampshire from 1882 to 1890. Conan Doyle first became interested in the supernatural about 1885 when he was invited to take part in table-turning seances at the house of a patient. He joined the Society for Psychical Research and carried out experiments in telepathy. He soon became convinced that telepathy was a fact, but was not sure about survival after death until later. In about 1900 Doyle gave up his career as a novelist and began to travel and lecture on Spiritualism in North America, Australia, New Zealand, and Europe. He was nicknamed "The St. Paul of Spiritualism" because of his zealous work. In 1925 Conan Doyle was nominated honorary president of the International Spiritual Congress, and was also president of the London Spiritualist Alliance. In his book *The Vital Message* (1919) Doyle wrote: "The physical basis of all psychic belief is that the soul is a complete duplicate of the body, resembling it in the smallest particular, although constructed of some far more tenuous material. In ordinary conditions these two bodies are intermingled so that the identity of the finer one is entirely obscured. At death, however, and under certain conditions, the two can divide and be seen separately." In 1926 he published *History of Spiritualism*, and since his death many mediums claim to have received messages from him.

DUNNE, JOHN WILLIAM (1875–1949)

British airplane designer who developed a new theory about time. The son of General Sir John Hart Dunne, he served in the Boer War and World War I, and designed Britain's first military plane in 1906–7. From about 1889 Dunne became interested in dreams, and started writing down his own experiences. His dreams were not very unusual until in 1916 he had a "night vision" of an explosion in a London bomb factory. In January 1917 such an explosion occurred, with 73 workers killed and more than 1000 injured. To explain the apparent prophetic nature of some dreams, Dunne worked out a philosophical theory that he explained in *Experiment with Time* (1927), *The Serial Universe* (1934), and *The New Immortality* (1938). After publication of the first book, Dunne was flooded with letters from readers who claimed to have had similar clairvoyant dreams. Dunne's basic theory was that human beings experience time on several different levels. The first "me," or Observer I, lives in the accepted flow of time, which moves from the past into the present into the future. But another "me," or Observer II, lives to the side of Observer I. In the ordinary waking state, Observer II is observing the "brain states" of Observer I. But when Observer I is asleep, Observer II can move out of the everyday flow of time, and look backward or forward at past and future events. Usually Observer II is all at sea, and cannot concentrate properly, but occasionally will have clear prophetic visions. Dunne was convinced that humans are immortal, and he called *An Experiment With Time* "the first scientific argument for human immortality." His theories of time have influenced writers such as J. B. Priestley and W. Somerset Maugham.

EDDY, MARY BAKER (1821–1910)

Founder of the Christian Science Church, which teaches that illness, pain, and even death are illusions, and that healing takes place through prayer to God. Born in New Hampshire, Mary Baker Eddy was for many years a semi-invalid. Following a serious fall on the ice in 1866 she read the story of the palsied man in St. Matthew's Gospel, and claimed to have risen from her bed similarly healed. Mrs. Eddy was a patient of Phineas Quimby (1802–66), a mesmerist who later turned to mental healing and believed that "the doctor makes the disease." She was probably influenced by his ideas. In 1875 she wrote *Science and Health*, the basic textbook of Christian Science. Four years later she organized the Church of Christ, Scientist in Boston and became a minister. The movement grew rapidly. Today it has over 3100 churches and societies in 57 countries, and publishes the respected newspaper the *Christian Science Monitor*.

EDWARDS, HARRY (b. 1893)

Famous British healer and Spiritualist. Edwards first discovered he had the power of healing in the Middle East during World War I, but until 1935 he devoted his energies to his family's printing business. He was an amateur magician and began attending Spiritualist meetings because he thought he could reproduce psychic phenomena by trickery. Instead he was convinced of the authenticity of psychic phenomena. Upon finding that he had special healing power, he has since the 1930s treated many thousands of people, some of whom had incurable illnesses. He uses spirit guides, including Louis Pasteur and Lord Lister, the famous English 19th-century surgeon. Edwards believes he can cure people both by the physical laying on of hands and by the power of thought at a distance. He wrote *Spirit Healing* (1960) and *The Power of Spiritual Healing* (1963).

Above: Mary Baker Eddy. In overcoming her own illness through faith and prayer, she inspired others to try the same way of being healed. She founded the Christian Science Church, which follows her teachings, in 1879.

Left: Harry Edwards, a leading British faith healer, frequently demonstrates his powers at public meetings. He treated this woman patient in Leeds, England in 1964.

EVA, C (Carrière, also known as Martha Beraud)

A French medium, famous for her apparent ability to materialize bodies and produce ectoplasm. She was the daughter of a French army officer and lived in Algeria at the beginning of the 20th century. Her psychic powers were discovered by General Noel and his wife, the parents of her fiancé who died in the Congo before they could marry. The Noels were extremely interested in psychic research and held many experimental seances with Eva C, as she became known. Eva C's control was Bien Boa, a Brahmin Hindu who had died about 300 years ago, and who claimed to be the spiritual guide of the Noel family. Charles Richet, professor of physiology in Paris, a Nobel prize winner, and leading French psychic researcher, was invited to investigate Eva C and held many seances at the Noel's villa in Algiers. During these seances Professor Richet reported that he saw a "kind of liquid or pasty jelly" emerging from Eva C's mouth and breast to form itself into the shape of a face or limb. This was the so-called "ectoplasm" that usually flies back into the medium's body if touched or exposed to light. It was claimed that Bien Boa appeared at these sessions five or six times, wearing white robes and a helmet. Professor Richet believed that the phenomena he had witnessed were genuine, and caused a sensation by publishing his finding in 1906. Between 1909 and 1918 Eva C was carefully studied by Baron von Schrenk Notzing, a German physician interested in psychic research, and by Dr. Gustave Geley, a French psychic researcher. She spent two months in London, but out of 40 seances given for the Society for Psychical Research, half were entirely blank and the rest weak. Skeptics put forward the theory that Eva C produced ectoplasm by regurgitating paper and fabric. She was one of the most controversial mediums of the early 20th century, and it was never proved whether or not she was a fraud.

Below: the controversial medium Eva C produced this human head from her own left ear. The substance of such materializations was given the name of ectoplasm.

Right: a scene from *Faust*, still one of the world's popular grand operas nearly 100 years after it was first presented. Written by Charles Gounod, it is based on Goethe's famous version of the legend of a medieval magician who sold his soul to the Devil.

Below: Colonel Percy Fawcett, British army officer who went on a search for the lost continent of Atlantis. Fawcett believed it to lie under the jungles of Brazil.

FAUST, or DR. FAUSTUS (1491–1540)

A German magician who may or may not actually have lived, but whose legend inspired many works of literature and music. The Faust story is based on the book *Historia von D. Johann Faustus* by Johann Spies (1587). Its hero was said to be the son of German peasants, born near the Weimar and brought up by a wealthy uncle who sent him to university. He took degrees in medicine and divinity, but also began to practice magic and, according to legend, sold his soul to the Devil in exchange for riches and power. Contemporaries described the person who may have been the real Faust as a coarse boastful man who cast horoscopes and was driven out of town for homosexuality and necromancy (foretelling the future by communication with the dead). The Faust legend was perpetuated in Christopher Marlowe's play *Dr. Faustus* (1604), Goethe's *Faust*, operas by Gounod and Busoni, and other musical works.

FAWCETT, COLONEL PERCY (1867–1925)

English explorer who believed that the ruins of Atlantis or cities built by Atlantean refugees lay beneath the jungles of Brazil. Col. Fawcett was born in Torquay, England, and joined the army when he was 19. He served in Ceylon and Hong Kong, and then was given an assignment on behalf of the Bolivian government. On exploring the Mato Grosso region of Brazil, he said he had been given a 150-year-old map drawn by a man who had found a lost city deep in the jungle. In 1925 Col. Fawcett, his eldest son Jack, and a friend Raleigh Rimell, started searching for this city, which they were sure had links with Atlantis. After a message from their camp in the Xingu Basin, the explorers disappeared. Some believed they had died of fever or had been killed by Indians; others thought they had found the lost city and stayed there. Two automatic writing mediums, Geraldine Cummins and E. Beatrice Gibbes, received messages from Col.

Above: a 17th-century manuscript entitled *The Alchemy of Flamel*, based on the work of the Frenchman who had lived some 200 years before. Flamel wrote that he had succeeded in the transmutation of ordinary metal into pure gold.

Fawcett after his disappearance. According to one communication, Fawcett had found pyramids in the jungle, and under the influence of drugs had traveled back in time. The people of the ancient Brazilian civilization, he said, had worshipped the sun and discovered a form of lighting akin to electricity. In 1948 Fawcett communicated that he was dead.

FICINO, MARSILIO (1433–99)
Italian philosopher, priest, and doctor who also wrote a textbook of magical medicine. Ficino led the Renaissance revival of interest in Plato's theories, and devoted most of his life to translating and interpreting Plato's works. Ficino believed that the universe is a hierarchy of substances ranging from God to inanimate matter, and that the human soul is immortal, an idea which had been neglected during the Middle Ages. His book gave instructions on making talismans or charms for medical use as protection against unfavorable planetary influences.

FLAMEL, NICHOLAS (about 1330–1419)
French alchemist. Born in Pontoise, Flamel was a scribe and copier of manuscripts and documents in Paris. In 1357 he came into possession of a very old manuscript made from thin leaves of bark which he referred to as *The Book of Abraham the Jew*. It contained instructions for the later stages of the transmutation of base metals into gold, but it gave no clue as to the essential first stage. After years of searching and experimenting Flamel records that in January 1382, he changed mercury into

pure silver, and three months later made his first transmutation into gold. Flamel apparently made a great fortune, which he gave to churches and charity. After Flamel had died many people thought that the Philosopher's Stone, used for transmuting metal into gold, was hidden in one of his houses. The townspeople, including the local magistrate, made a thorough search of Flamel's property, but there is no record of anything being found. However, they nearly ruined the house in the process of searching. Some insisted that Flamel, having discovered the secret of the Philosopher's Stone, had also found the key to immortality, and after his death several people claimed they met him.

FODOR, DR. NANDOR (1895–1964)

Hungarian-born psychoanalyst and psychic researcher. Fodor studied law at the Royal Hungarian University of Science. In 1921 he went to the United States as staff reporter on a Hungarian daily paper in New York. He became interested in the supernatural after finding Hereward Carrington's book *Modern Psychic Phenomena* in a New York bookshop. Fodor became a friend of Carrington and together they wrote *Story of the Poltergeist Down the Ages*. In 1929 Fodor moved to England where he worked for Lord Rothermere, owner of a chain of newspapers. In 1934 he became assistant editor of *Light*, the oldest British Spiritualist journal, and took part in research into levitation, hauntings, poltergeists, and materialization. Fodor first became interested in psychiatry when he interviewed Sandor Ferenczi, an associate of Freud, in New York, and he came to believe that psychoanalysis could throw light on psychic phenomena. In 1936 he investigated the Ash Manor Ghost and the Thornton Heath Poltergeist, and suggested that the Ash Manor hauntings took place because of abnormal sexual relationships in the family concerned. Fodor's frankness about sex was considered shocking in Britain in the 1930s, and as a result he was dismissed from his post as Research Officer of the International Institute for Psychical Research. Fodor's most important book was *Encyclopaedia of Psychic Science* (1934).

FORTUNE, DION (1891–1946)

British magician and founder of the Fraternity of the Inner Light, a successor to the Order of the Golden Dawn. Dion's real name was Violet Mary Firth. Her parents were Christian Scientists, and her interest in supernatural powers sprang from early contact with the teachings of Mary Baker Eddy. Dion Fortune believed that malevolent people can consciously or unconsciously vampirize another person, causing the astral body to leak vital energy. Following her subjection to great emotional strain by the principal of a school where she worked, Dion was a mental and physical wreck for three years. She then studied psychology and occultism in order to learn how to counter such situations, which she called a "psychic attack." She joined the Alpha and Omega Lodge of the Stella Matutina, an offshoot of the Golden Dawn led by Mrs. McGregor Mathers, widow of a founder of the original Golden Dawn. She became convinced that Mrs. Mathers was also attacking her psychically by filling

Above: Kate Fox, youngest of the three sisters whose communication with the dead as mediums led to the founding of Spiritualism. In 1888, she followed her sister Margaret in confessing to fraud. Below: the home of the Foxes in Hydesville, New York, reconstructed as a shrine to mark the start of Spiritualism there in 1848.

her house with cats. In trance, Dion Fortune met Mrs. Mathers on the astral plane and survived a psychic battle with her. She described "psychic vampirism" in her famous book *Psychic Self-Defense*. She also wrote *The Mystical Quabalah*, regarded by many as a classic, *The Cosmic Doctrine*, and several novels with supernatural themes including *The Demon Lover, The Sea Priestess* and *Moon Magic*.

FOX sisters, KATE (1841–1892), MARGARET (1838–1893), and LEAH (1814–1890)

American mediums and pioneers of Spiritualism. In 1848 mysterious raps and noises began to disturb the Fox family in their cottage in Hydesville, New York, which already had a reputation for mysterious happenings. The two little girls, Kate and Margaret, devised a method of communicating with the unseen presence, asking questions that were answered with one rap for "yes," and two raps for "no." The answers revealed that the body of a murdered man lay beneath the cottage, and John Fox, father of the three sisters, later claimed that he found fragments of hair and bones under the cellar floor. When Kate moved to her brother's house in Auburn, New York, and Margaret to her married sister's house in Rochester, New York, the raps broke out in both houses. A tenant in the Rochester house of Leah became the center of poltergeist activity, with things being thrown at him. Leah became the first professional medium, and the Fox family began to hold seances during which the table

rocked, objects moved, a guitar seemingly played by itself, and sitters felt the touch of invisible hands. The first meeting of people calling themselves Spiritualists was held in the Corinthian Hall, Rochester, on November 14, 1849. Local reaction was partly hostile and a committee was formed to investigate, but no fraud was uncovered. In the 1850s Margaret and Leah retired from public life for a while, but their younger sister Kate continued to hold seances, producing spirit forms as well as raps. For five years Kate was employed as a private medium by Charles F. Livermore, a rich New York banker who wanted to contact his dead wife Estelle. In 1871 Livermore arranged for Kate to visit England, where she was investigated by Sir William Crookes, the British scientist, and where she held joint sittings with the well-known mediums Daniel Dunglas Home and Mrs. Samuel Guppy. In May 1888 Margaret Fox, who was an alcoholic and had quarreled with Leah, published a confession saying that it was "all fraud, hypocrisy, and delusion," and in October 1888 Kate made a similar confession. A year later Margaret retracted her confession. Despite the confessions, the drama, and the scandal of the Fox sisters' last years, Spiritualism survived and grew.

FOX, OLIVER (b. 1885)
British astral projector who had studied science and engineering. Fox was a sickly child, and from an early age had had strange dreams, including a recurrent nightmare in which he saw his mother and her double. From about the year 1913 he developed the ability to control his dreams and project his astral body through the "pineal doorway," the unused "eye" in the center of the brain, that occult tradition says is the opening to other states of being. The method he used was to prolong a dream. This would result in severe pain, but as this diminished, he would hear a click. His consciousness would then be transferred to the place of his dream, and he was able to leave his body and fly through the air, passing through walls and other obstacles. His experiences are described in the *Occult Review* of 1920, and in his own book *Astral Projection*, published in 1962.

FREUD, SIGMUND (1856–1939)
Austrian-Jewish founder of psychoanalysis, who described dreams as the "royal road to the unconscious." He believed dreams represented the fulfillment of repressed desires. Freud set out his theories in *The Interpretation of Dreams* (1900), which he considered his most important work. He contended that during sleep the ego relaxes its control over unacceptable impulses, but it exercises a form of censorship so that dreams often appear in a symbolic and distorted form. When a sleeper wakes up, the conscious mind changes the dream again by giving order and coherence to the remembered fragments of a dream experience. For Freud, the symbols in dreams were primarily sexual in meaning, although he also saw evidence of other repressed desires. He believed that the hidden content of his patients' dreams could be revealed by "free association" of ideas during psychoanalysis, and that dreams provided clues to the origins of a patient's neurosis.

Above: Sigmund Freud, the first doctor to use psychoanalysis in the treatment of mental distress or illness. His work on dreams and their meanings has had a deep influence on modern thinking.

GALL, FRANZ JOSEPH (1758–1828)

Physician and founder of phrenology, the practice of reading bumps on the head. Gall was born in Tiefenbrunn, Germany, and studied and practiced medicine in Vienna. As a boy he had noticed that the most outstanding scholars in his school had prominent eyes and certain peculiarities in the shape of their heads, and he formulated the theory that the different shapes were caused by variations in development of certain parts of the brain. After graduating from university Gall spent several years visiting schools, prisons, and lunatic asylums, measuring hundreds of skulls with calipers. Between 1805 and 1807 he made a sensational lecture tour, explaining his theories amidst much scorn and mocking. In 1807 he settled in Paris. Phrenology fell into greater disrepute and Gall suffered financial and social hardship.

GARDNER, GERALD BROUSSEAU (1884–1964)

British rubber planter and customs official who revived witchcraft in England in the 1950s. After spending much of his life in the Far East, Gardner returned to Britain in the late 1930s, and according to him, discovered a group of witches in the New Forest. He believed that witchcraft was the pagan Old Religion of Europe, a theory already suggested by the anthropologist Dr. Margaret Murray. In the 1940s Gardner was in touch with many groups of self-styled witches, and said he was initiated into witchcraft in 1946. He dabbled in Spiritualism, anthropology, and folklore and had unorthodox sexual tastes. The Gardnerian

Below: Franz Joseph Gall. Once a successful doctor, he became a laughing stock after he developed phrenology as a way to determine human character through the study of irregular shapes on the head.

Below right: this 19th-century English ceramic head shows the divisions of the brain as used for phrenological readings of people.

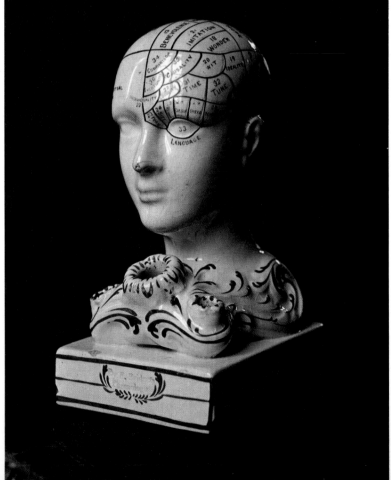

witch cult included rituals involving nudity, scourging, and copulation. In 1954 Gardner published *Witchcraft Today*, a restatement of many of Dr. Murray's ideas, and in 1959 he wrote *The Meaning of Witchcraft*.

GARRETT, EILEEN J. (1893–1970)

Famous Irish-born medium. Eileen Garrett began her career in Britain as a trance medium, and in 1930 she was invited to the National Laboratory of Psychical Research in London. She was asked to try to contact the spirit of Sir Arthur Conan Doyle, the famous author of *Sherlock Holmes*, who had died recently. But when Mrs. Garrett went into a trance, sitters heard instead the voice of Flight Lieutenant H. Carmichael Irwin, pilot of the airship R. 101, which had crashed in France two days before killing most of the passengers and crew. Flight Lieutenant Irwin gave details of the crash, and these were taken down in shorthand. They were sent to the Air Ministry, which later confirmed that parts of the message tallied in every detail with the report of the official enquiry. In 1932–33 Mrs. Garrett went on a tour of the United States, and later became an American citizen. She herself was uncertain about the nature of psychic gifts and phenomena in general and her own in particular. She suspected that her spirit controls were really factors in her own mind. She was subjected to psychoanalytical tests at Johns Hopkins University, Baltimore, and at the New York Psychiatric Institute, and these went a long way to prove the independent personality of her spirit controls. She founded the Parapsychology Foundation in New York in 1951 to promote research, and wrote *My Life as a Search for the Meaning of Mediumship* (1938), *Adventures in the Supernormal* (1949) and *Many Voices* (1968). Eileen Garrett also had out-of-body experiences while in trance. She was able to report what she had seen, and her presence was felt by people whom she visited during astral projection.

GAUQUELIN, MICHEL ROLAND (b. 1928)

French psychologist and statistician who has found a positive relationship between the position of the planets at birth and the professions later chosen by eminent people. Michel Gauquelin was born in Paris, the son of a dental surgeon. He got a diploma at the Institute of Psychology, Paris University, and studied statistics at the Sorbonne. From the age of about seven he was interested in astrology, and in 1950 began research to disprove the claims of the astrologers. He examined the statistical evidence of several well-known astrologers and showed that their conclusions were based on very small test groups or faulty mathematics. Then he ran tests of his own, examining the horoscopes of thousands of professional men. To his surprise he found that doctors were often born under the influence of Mars or Saturn, military men under Mars or Jupiter, politicians and athletes under Mars, and journalists and actors under Jupiter. The odds against links occurring simply by chance ranged from one million to 50 million to one. Later Gauquelin studied 30,000 parents and children, and found that children are frequently born under the same or similar planetary influences as their parents. He suggested that some elemnt in the genetic make-up may be subject

Above: Gerald Gardner, British self-proclaimed witch who led a revival of witchcraft in the 1950s. He emphasized sexual magic rather than ceremonial magic, which is the more common form at present.

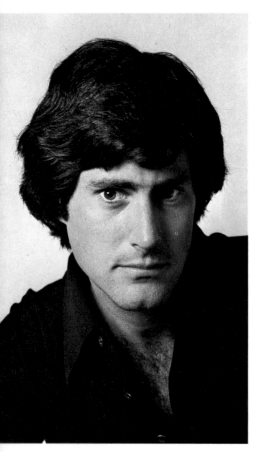

Above: Uri Geller, one of the most famous and controversial psychics living today. He has been much investigated by scientists, especially for his spoon-bending skill.

to cosmic influences, helping to determine when a person is born and what the future will be like. In 1969 Gauquelin became director of an organization investigating cosmic psychophysiological relationships. He has written: *The Scientific Basis of Astrology, Cosmic Influences on Human Behavior, How Atmospheric Conditions Affect Your Health,* and, with his wife Françoise, *Psychology in the 20th Century.*

GELLER, URI (b. 1946)
Israeli psychic. Geller was born in Tel Aviv, the son of Jewish immigrants from Hungary. He discovered his telepathic powers at the age of three, and as a schoolboy found he had the skill to bend and break metal by gently rubbing it or concentrating on it. After serving in the Israeli army in the Six Day War, Geller started giving public demonstrations of his skills. He has appeared on television many times in Europe and the United States, and has been investigated by several scientists including Professor John Taylor of London University. In Professor Taylor's laboratory in 1974 Geller deflected a needle on a geiger counter by holding the counter in his hands and concentrating on it. Geller has written his autobiography, called *My Story.*

GRANT, JOAN (b. 1907)
Author of many books about her previous lives. Born in London, Joan Grant was educated privately by governesses and tutors. As a child she realized she had memories of former lives in other centuries and other countries. A visit to Egypt brought back detailed impressions of life in that land thousands of years ago. In 1936, at the age of 29, Joan Grant learned the technique of reliving previous incarnations as a deliberate exercise. In 1937 she put memories of one incarnation together in the form of a novel, *Winged Pharaoh,* which describes the life of Sekeeta, the daughter of an Egyptian pharaoh who lived 3000 years ago. Memories of other incarnations were described in *Eyes of Horus* (1942); *Life as Carola* (1939); *Redskin Morning and Other Stories* (1944); and an autobiography, *Far Memory,* which also appeared as *Time Out of Mind* (1956). Joan Grant believes that she had at least four Egyptian childhoods, and that *Redskin Morning* recalls a North American reincarnation 2000 years B.C. Her third husband, Dr. Denys Kelsey, is a psychiatrist who became interested in reincarnation when using age-regression hypnosis in the treatment of patients. They have been working together since 1958. In 1967 they were co-authors of *Many Lifetimes.*

GUPPY, MRS. SAMUEL, also Agnes Nichol before marriage (died 1917)
British medium who had worked as a professional hypnotist when she was a young girl. Mrs. Guppy was most famous for *apportation*—that is, the production of objects such as live lobsters and eels, fresh fruit, flowers, and vegetables apparently from nowhere. At one seance the Duchess of Arpino requested sea sand. It appeared, together with sea water and live starfish, although the sea was about 100 yards away. Another time Princess Marguerite of Naples asked for specimens of a prickly cactus, and more than 20 appeared. On June 3, 1871, when two

other mediums were holding a joint seance with eight sitters at 61 Lamb's Conduit Street, London, someone jokingly suggested that the spirits bring Mrs. Guppy to the seance from her house three miles away. It is claimed that the bulky Mrs. Guppy arrived with a bump on the table, her shoes off and in a trance.

GURDJIEFF, GEORGEI IVANOVITCH (about 1872–1949)

Russian mystic and founder of the Institute for the Harmonious Development of Man. Gurdjieff was born of Greek parents in Alexandropol (now Leninakan) in the Causasus. In his youth he traveled widely, visiting Asia, Africa, and Europe, in search of spiritual truth. During his travels he studied the techniques of yoga and met dervishes and fakirs. He returned to Russia and in 1917 founded the Institute for the Harmonious Development of Man in the Caucasus, where he taught his theories. Gurdjieff's elaborate system of philosophy and psychological development was known to his pupils as "The Work." His basic idea was that people are usually asleep, little more than machines, but that with discipline and "super-effort" they can gain control of the enormous reserves of energy that exist in all humans, but which are normally tapped only in moments of crisis. Gurdjieff's admirers believed that he had psychic powers, and that he was able to revitalize his followers by telepathic communication of energy. During the Russian Revolution he led expeditions through dangerous countryside in which they had to make the "super-effort" that Gurdjieff believed gave people great power. Political conditions in the Soviet Union forced Gurdjieff and his followers to move to Constantinople, where they continued their work. In 1922 Gurdjieff set up his Institute at Prieure des Basses Loges, a chateau in Fountainbleau near Paris. There his disciples lived spartan lives, did ceaseless manual work, and gained physical and mental control of themselves by practicing Gurdjieff's "dervish dances," among other exercises. Gurdjieff's pupils were bound to secrecy, and nothing was published about his work until after his death. Then, two of his books, *All and Everything* and *Meetings With Remarkable Men*, as well as writings by his followers, achieved a wide circulation.

Above: Georgei Gurdjieff, modern cult figure whose system of mental and physical exercises was designed to awaken the latent powers he felt exist in us all.

GURNEY, EDMUND (1847–88)

A founder and Secretary of the Society for Psychical Research, and Fellow of Trinity College, Cambridge. The son of a clergyman, Gurney studied classics, music, and medicine, but never took up a profession and devoted much of his life to the work of the SPR. He was particularly interested in telepathy, especially the difference between cases in which the image received was the same as that in the agent's mind, and those in which the percipient sees something different from the agent, such as an image of the agent himself. He thought there was a possible physical basis in the first instances, but none in the second. Gurney also studied hallucinations and the psychological side of hypnotism, and wrote *Phantasms of the Living* (1886) with F. W. H. Myers and Frank Podmore, also founder members of the SPR. After his death automatic writers such as the mediums Mrs. A. W. Verrall and Mrs. Holland claimed to have received communications from him.

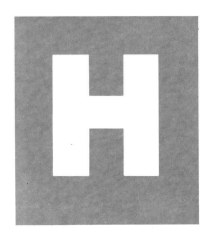

HEUVELMANS, DR. BERNARD (b. 1916)

French-born zoologist who believes that some of the mythical monsters of land and sea may have existed, or still exist. His book *On the Track of Unknown Animals* (1958) examines evidence for fabulous creatures from the spotted lion of Kenya and the Queensland marsupial tiger, which are almost admitted to the official catalog of zoology, to the more mysterious Abominable Snowman, or Yeti, and the monstrous snakes reported in the Amazon. Dr. Heuvelmans concludes: "The world is by no means thoroughly explored. It is true that there are no more large islands or continents to be discovered. But because a country is on the map it does not mean that we know all about its inhabitants." In another book, *In the Wake of Sea Serpents* (1969), Dr. Heuvelmans traces the stories about sea serpents from ancient to modern times. He mentions the giant squid, or kraken, a "mythical" beast which in fact was caught and classified as "architeuthis monachus" in 1857. "If Nature had thrown the dice differently the sea serpent might be the known animal and the kraken still a beast of legend," he writes. Dr. Heuvelmans has a degree in zoological sciences from Brussels University, and has made many television appearances in Britain and Europe. He is known in France as the "Sherlock Holmes of zoology."

HODGSON, DR. RICHARD (1855–1905)

Member of the British Society for Psychical Research who spent many years investigating psychic phenomena. Dr. Hodgson was born in Melbourne, Australia, and studied law at Cambridge University, England. His legal training made him particularly adept at detecting fraud. He joined the SPR in 1882 and became a member of the Council in 1885. In 1884 Hodgson went to India to investigate Madame Blavatsky's psychic activities, and declared her a fraud. He was very skeptical about psychic phenomena and said that "nearly all professional mediums form a gang of vulgar tricksters, more or less in league with one another." He was convinced that the Italian medium, Eusapia Paladino, was an imposter. However, after Hodgson spent 15 years studying Mrs. Leonore Piper's career as a medium in the United States, his attitudes to Spiritualism slowly changed. He decided that Mrs. Piper was genuine, and that spirits must be communicating through her.

HOME, DANIEL DUNGLAS (1833–86)

One of the best-known mediums in the history of Spiritualism. Born in Scotland, he was adopted by a childless aunt who later took him to the United States. He is said to have had his first vision at the age of 13 when a friend who had died appeared to him in a cloud. Soon rappings began to occur in his presence. His aunt believed he was possessed by the Devil and called in an assortment of Christian ministers to exorcise the spirits. However, the rappings continued and finally she turned Home out of the house. From then on he seems to have lived on the hospitality of admiring friends. Home's first levitation took place at the house of an American manufacturer, and witnesses heard strains of music although there was no instrument nearby. At the age of 22 he went to London and won immediate fame through the strange happenings at his seances. At one sitting he floated out of a third story window and in at another. He caused tables to move and accordions to play by themselves. Knockings and rappings apparently conveyed messages from the dead, and mysterious moving hands would often appear. Sir William Crookes, the scientist and psychic researcher, subjected Home to the most rigorous tests that could be devised, and became convinced that Home's powers were genuine. He wrote: "Of all persons endowed with a powerful development of this Psychic Force, Mr. Daniel Dunglas Home is the most remarkable." Unlike most mediums, Home was never detected in fraud.

HÖRBIGER, HANNS (1860–1931)

Austrian engineer who invented Glacial Cosmology, a theory of the universe that greatly interested Hitler, Himmler, and other Nazi leaders. According to Hörbiger, the universe is filled with "cosmic building stuff" consisting of hot metallic stars and "cosmic ice." When a block of ice plunges into a hot star, an explosion is set off. This generates a stellar system. He also believed that the lands of Atlantis and Lemuria sank when the earth "captured" the moon in the past. He said that the earth had had several moons, and their collision with our planet caused the catastrophes recorded in legends of the Flood, the Twilight of the Gods, and the Book of Revelation. In 1892 Hörbiger had a vision that gave him a clue to the meaning of the universe. In 1906 he convinced Philipp Fauth, an amateur astronomer, that his cosmic theory made sense, and together they published *Glacial Cosmology*. Hörbiger's theories appealed to supporters of Atlantis, who sought an explanation for the disappearance of Atlantis under the sea. The German national *volkisch* (folklore) movement, which believed that the original Aryan "master race" had arisen in Atlantis, took Hörbiger to its heart. Himmler used to send Cosmic Ice literature to high-ranking Nazi officials, and Hitler declared that when he created his ideal city in his birthplace, Linz, he would erect an observatory dedicated to Hörbiger. Even today Hörbiger's Cosmic Ice Theory has thousands of supporters.

HOUDINI, HARRY, born Erich Weiss (1874–1926)

Magician and world-famous escape artist who used his skills to expose fraudulent mediums. Born in Appleton, Wisconsin, he began to do rigorous exercises while very young to develop muscle control. He became a trapeze artist. By 1889 he had perfected a "challenge act" in which he guaranteed to escape from virtually any set of handcuffs, from straitjackets, padlocked boxes, and prison cells. Other famous acts that he devised were the "water torture cell" in which he was submerged upside down in a tank full of water with his feet securely padlocked to an iron grid at the top of the tank; and "walking through a wall" in which he apparently passed through an impenetrable wall of steel. His many successful escapes brought him international fame. Houdini achieved them through a mixture of fantastic physical dexterity, a lifetime's study of locks, and an element of trickery. However, Houdini never claimed to be more than an entertainer, and he conducted a long crusade against mediums,

Below: a portrait of Daniel Dunglas Home, one of the greatest mediums in history. He was subjected to many closely controlled tests, none of which ever proved him fraudulent. At one time in his life he was told by the spirits that he would lose his powers for a year, and he did. But he regained them in exactly one year.

EUROPE'S ECLIPSING SENSATION
HOUDINI
THE WORLD'S HANDCUFF KING & PRISON BREAKER
"NOTHING ON EARTH CAN HOLD HOUDINI A PRISONER"

exposing many of them as frauds through his own skills. He starred in silent films and wrote several books, among which *Miracle Mongers and their Methods* (1920) and *A Magician among the Spirits* (1924) are the best known.

HURKOS, PETER, born Pieter van der Hurk (b. 1911)

Dutch psychometrist born in Dordrecht, the Netherlands. He fell 36 feet in 1941, landing on his head and shoulders. For three days he was unconscious in the hospital, and when he recovered, he discovered he had a psychic ability to know things about people by touching objects that belonged to them. After leaving the hospital Hurkos returned to working for the Dutch resistance movement. He was caught with forged papers and shipped to the notorious concentration camp at Buchenwald. By 1946 he was demonstrating his psychometric powers at theaters in Europe, and in 1956 was taken to the United States by the psychic researcher Andrija Puharich. Hurkos has helped the American police to reconstruct crimes by using his psychometric powers. He was called in on the cases of the Boston Strangler and the Sharon Tate murders.

JUNG, CARL GUSTAV (1875–1961)

Distinguished Swiss psychiatrist who also studied and wrote about alchemy, clairvoyance, flying saucers, and other occult subjects. Jung became interested in Spiritualism while studying medicine at Basel University, and the material he gathered formed the basis of his doctoral thesis. He was at first a disciple of the psychiastrist Sigmund Freud, but later broke away from him. Jung's psychology is based on the theory that the mind has three parts consisting of the conscious, the personal unconscious, and the collective or racial unconscious. The last-named contains archetypes, or images, derived from the distilled memories of the human species. These archetypes appear in symbolic form in dreams and mythology. Jung believed that people achieve spiritual wholeness and self-fulfillment by coming to terms with the elements in their unconscious minds. Jung disagreed with Freud's theory that dreams are preoccupied with sexual wishes and frustrations. He believed that dreams may also "give expression to ineluctable truths, to philosophical pronouncements, illusions, wild fantasies . . . and heaven knows what besides." Many dreams, he thought, reflect the perennial archetypal myths of the human race. Jung studied alchemy for many years, and in *Psychology and Alchemy* he put forward the idea that alchemy was a symbol of the human attempt to achieve a higher state of perfection. He noticed that many alchemical symbols occurred in the dreams of his patients, and in mythology and religion. He thought these symbols stemmed from the collective unconscious, and that they might provide a clue to our true nature. Jung was also interested in meaningful coincidences, which he called "synchronicity." Jung felt this synchronicity or coincidence somehow had its roots in powerful unconscious mental processes. He used the *I Ching*, the ancient Chinese text of divination, with some of his patients, and was amazed how often the revelations of the Chinese oracle bore startling resemblance to the patients' dreams or psychological states.

KELLEY, EDWARD (1555?–1594?)

British scryer and alchemist. According to Kelley he was born Edward Talbot in Worcester and studied at Oxford University without taking a degree. He became an apothecary's apprentice and notary, then turned to forging and counterfeiting, for which his ears were clipped. Kelley claimed that an innkeeper near Bristol sold him a bottle of red powder and a document in the Celtic language, which he deciphered and found to be a treatise on alchemy. In 1582 he met Dr. John Dee, the scholar and astrologer, and was employed as his scryer. Later Kelley and Dee traveled abroad, and Kelley used his red powder to perform apparent transmutations of metal into gold. Gradually his stock of powder dwindled and he immersed himself in the study of alchemy, determined to renew his supply. Dee left him to return to England and Kelley finally was imprisoned by Emperor Rudolf of Bohemia on charges of sorcery and heresy. While in prison the first time, Kelley wrote his treatise *The Stone of the Philosophers.*

KEYHOE, MAJOR DONALD EDWARD (b. 1897)

Best-selling American author of books on flying saucers. Major Keyhoe is a graduate of the United States Naval Academy, and during World War II was a Marine aircraft and balloon pilot. Major Keyhoe caused a sensation in 1949 when he wrote the article "Flying Saucers Are Real" for *True* magazine. In it he claimed that the United States Air Force was concealing the truth about flying saucers. For many years Keyhoe was director of the National Investigative Committee on Aerial Phenomena. His flying saucer books include *Flying Saucers are Real, Flying Saucers from Outer Space, The Flying Saucer Conspiracy,* and *Flying Saucers—Top Secret.*

Below: the aura of a plant as revealed by Kirlian photography, a system of taking pictures in high-frequency electrical fields. Developed by Semyon and Valentina Kirlian in the Soviet Union, the process has shown that animals and plants have colored haloes.

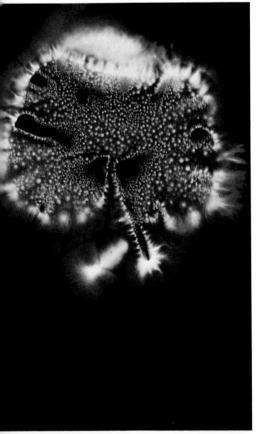

KIRLIAN, SEMYON AND VALENTINA

Soviet scientists who developed a process called Kirlian photography through which the colored auras surrounding living organisms is revealed. In 1939 Semyon Kirlian was working as an electrical engineer, while his wife Valentina was a teacher and journalist. One day he was called into the local research unit and watched a demonstration of a high frequency instrument used for electrotherapy. As the patient was treated Kirlian noticed a small flash of light between an electrode and the patient's skin. Working alone in their two-room apartment, the Kirlians began to develop instruments that could take photographs of organisms placed in high-frequency electrical fields. Kirlian photography has revealed that animals and plants are haloed by luminous flares, and that the size and color of these vary according to the physical and emotional state of the subject. One photograph revealed a ghostlike aura in the area where part of a leaf had been cut off. Soviet and American scientists became interested in the photographic process and verified the findings of Kirlian photography. In 1968 six Soviet scientists led by Dr. Vladimir Inyushin suggested that living organisms not only have a physical body made of atoms and molecules, but also a "bioplasmic body" that is identical to the aura or astral body described by mediums and other occultists.

MANSON, CHARLES (b. 1935)

Leader of a California commune that indulged in sexual orgies, drugs, and strange religious practices, and finally became involved in the notorious Sharon Tate murder and other murders. Manson spent many of his early years in corrective institutions and prisons, and was described by a psychiatrist in 1959 as "very unstable emotionally and very insecure." During a period at McNeil Island Penitentiary, Manson began studying magic, astral projection, hypnotism, and scientology. On release from prison, Manson gathered a "family" of disciples, mostly young women, whom he frequently beat up and forced to take part in sadistic sexual practices. The Family set up a commune·at the Spahn movie ranch in the San Fernando Valley, California, and later in Death Valley. The women in the Family believed that Manson was Jesus Christ, although he never claimed this. He did say, however, that he had lived 2000 years ago and had died on a cross, and he also referred to himself as the Devil, or Satan, or Soul. The Family returned to the Spahn ranch in 1969, when it is said that Manson made a deliberate decision to kill. His followers plundered the San Fernando Valley, stealing cars, robbing service stations, and on one occasion removing a load of fruit and vegetables from a refrigerated truck after drugging the driver. On August 8, 1969, members of The Family brutally murdered movie actress Sharon Tate and four companions at a secluded house near Los Angeles, and the next night killed supermarket chain owner Leon LaBianca and his wife. Manson was convicted of masterminding the murders.

MATHERS, SAMUEL LIDDELL McGREGOR (1854–1918)

British occultist and leader of the Order of the Golden Dawn, which he helped found in 1888 with Dr. William Wynn Westcott and Dr. William Woodman. An extremely eccentric man, Mathers adopted the name of Count McGregor of Glenstrae and frequently wore full Scottish Highland dress. He claimed to be in direct contact with the Secret Chiefs, semi-divine spirits who dictated new rituals to him through his wife, Mina, the daughter of the famous French philosopher Henri Bergson. Mathers spent a great deal of time in the British Museum copying magical texts. He also produced an English translation of *The Key of Solomon*, the most famous textbook of European ritual magic, and translated *The Book of the Sacred Magic of Abra-Melin the Mage* which had been printed in 1458, and *The Kabbalah Unveiled*. In 1892 Mathers quarreled with his employer and was dismissed from his job as curator of a private museum. He went to Paris with his wife, and tried to control the London-based Order of the Golden Dawn from France. Aleister Crowley supported McGregor when his leadership was challenged, but they later quarreled and put magic curses on each other. Crowley claimed that his curses were responsible for Mathers' death in 1918.

MESMER, FRANZ ANTON (1735–1815)

German doctor and discoverer of mesmerism, later known as hypnotism. Mesmer was born in Baden, Germany, studied medicine in Vienna, and wrote his doctoral thesis on the influence

Below: Charles Manson, notorious leader of the cult known as the Family, in which killing on his orders was an accepted way of life. He and his underlings were convicted and imprisoned for the brutal murder of actress Sharon Tate and friends, among others.

of the planets on human health. In 1773 Mesmer met a woman who believed that the application of magnets would cure her stomach pains. This idea seemed to support his own theory that there is some kind of vital fluid that flows like tides through the body, causing health or sickness, and that might be subject to magnetic influences. He began to use magnets on his own patients, and they seemed to work. However, while bleeding a patient one day, Mesmer noticed that the bleeding increased when he moved close, and decreased when he moved away. He thought this meant that he himself acted as some sort of magnet, and he coined the phrase "animal magnetism" to describe this kind of personal power. Mesmer's cures made him one of the most famous doctors in Vienna, and he began to experiment with "magnetized water," vats of water filled with iron filings into which metal rods were fixed. To the accompaniment of music, patients grasped the rods and moved about, finally going into trance or having a convulsion. Many were cured of their illnesses by this treatment. Mesmer moved to Paris in 1778 and had even greater success, but was denounced as a charlatan. When the French government ordered an enquiry into Mesmer's methods by doctors and scientists, they produced an adverse report and he fell into disrepute. Mesmer spent the last years of his life in Meersburg, Germany. A few years later one of Mesmer's disciples, the Marquis of Puysegur, tried to magnetize a shepherd boy by stroking his head, and to his surprise the boy went into a deep trancelike sleep. The Marquis had stumbled on hypnotism. Mesmer had in fact been using the power of suggestion on patients, probably without realizing it.

Above: a medallion of Franz Anton Mesmer, the doctor whose work as a healer led to the development of hypnotism in medical treatment. Below: a cartoon ridiculing Mesmer's treatment in his luxurious salon. Influenced by his "animal magnetism," patients fell into convulsions—and came out cured.

MESSING, WOLF

Polish psychic. Wolf Messing was a stage mind reader who fled from Poland to the Soviet Union during World War II. He was alleged to have remarkable telepathic powers. On one occasion, it is said, Messing walked into a bank, presented the cashier with a bank note, and willed him to hand over 100,000 roubles, which he did. In 1940 Stalin set a test for Messing. It was to attempt to "will" his way into the ruler's country house. One day as Stalin sat working in his office, Messing walked in past all the guards and servants, who had respectfully allowed him by. Messing's explanation was that he had willed the guards to think that he was Lavrenti Beria, the then head of the powerful Soviet secret police.

MIKHAILOVA, NELYA (b. 1927)

Soviet psychic who apparently "sees" with her fingers and can move small objects by the power of her mind. Nelya Mikhailova served in the Tank Regiment of the Red Army and took part in the defense of Leningrad against the Germans in World War II when she was only 14. A plump attractive woman with dark expressive eyes, Mrs. Mikhailova discovered her psychokinetic powers when recovering from battle injuries in the hospital at the end of the war. She recalls: "I was very angry one day and I was walking toward a cupboard when suddenly a pitcher moved to the edge of the shelf, fell, and smashed to bits." But unlike most people plagued by poltergeists, Nelya Mikhailova found she

could control the energy. Her psychokinetic powers were tested and confirmed by Edward Naumov, a biologist at Moscow State University, and other scientists. Dr. Gerady Sergeyev, a neurologist at the Utomski Institute, Leningrad, set up numerous tests which revealed among other things that Mrs. Mikhailova has a magnetic field surrounding her body only 10 times less than that of the earth itself. She also has an unusual brain wave pattern which generates 50 times more voltage from the back of her head than from the front, while most people generate only three to four times more. After psychokinetic experiments, such as one in which she separated the yolk from the white of an egg by will power, she loses several pounds in weight and is physically and emotionally exhausted. When convalescing in a Leningrad hospital in the 1960s, Nelya Mikhailova found she could "see" the colors of her embroidery threads with her fingertips, and these powers were later tested by Dr. Leonid Vasiliev, a Soviet pioneer in psychic research.

MONROE, ROBERT (b. 1915)
American researcher on out-of-the-body-experiences and author of *Journeys Out of the Body* (1971). Born in Indiana, Robert Monroe was a writer and producer of radio programs from 1937 to 1949, and is now president of several radio and electronics corporations. He had his first out-of-the-body-experience (OOBE) when he was a child, and from 1958 on these became increasingly frequent. In 1965–66 he took part in experiments at the Brain Wave Laboratory of the University of Virgina Medical School, and it was found that during his OOBEs his brain wave pattern was like that of dreaming sleep. He was not in a death-like trance. There was no change in his heart rate, but there was a fall in blood pressure. Monroe opened the Mind Research Institute at his farm in Virginia in 1971, and conducted further experiments in OOBE phenomena. It was found that an OOBE most frequently took place when a person was lying warm and relaxed on a bed, in a north–south position. In the successful experiments, about 40 percent were willfully induced; 15 percent were spontaneous, and 45 percent were indeterminate. In *Journeys out of the Body* Robert Monroe describes these experiments and also gives step-by-step instructions on how to project out of the body.

MULDOON, SYLVAN J.
American astral traveler. Muldoon had his first experience of astral projection when he was 12 years old and staying at a Spiritualist Association camp in Iowa. He woke and did not know where he was, tried to move, and found he was powerless. He described this state as "astral catalepsy." He felt himself floating toward the ceiling, still in a cataleptic state, and after two minutes was "uprighted" into a perpendicular position and found himself standing on the floor. He then felt free and was able to look at his physical body lying on the bed, attached to the astral body by an "elasticlike cable." He wandered around the house for 15 minutes, then felt the cable drawing him back to his physical body. Muldoon became an experienced astral projector. Often he later came upon places he had visited on an astral pro-

jection. After reading *Modern Psychical Phenomena*, which mentioned astral projection, Muldoon wrote to the author, Dr. Hereward Carrington, a well-known British psychic researcher. They met and together produced one of the most important studies of astral projection, *The Projection of the Astral Body* (1929).

MURRAY, DR. MARGARET (1863–1963)
British anthropologist and archeologist who believed that witchcraft can be traced back to the Old Religion, an ancient pre-Christian religion based on worship of the Great Mother and the Horned God, primitive symbols of fertility and power. In 1921 Dr. Murray set out her theory in *The Witch-Cult in Western Europe,* and followed this book with *The God of the Witches* and *The Divine King in England.* Many scholars refute her thesis, but agree that her books encouraged the revival of witchcraft in 20th-century England. Dr. Murray suggested that the late medieval and Renaissance witch hunts were the outcome of a conflict between Christianity and an organized counterreligion. She held that the Old Religion, or Dianic Cult as she called it, had its own hierarchy, witches' covens, and festivals as late as the 17th century. She believed that some of the English kings were high-ranking members of the cult. Dr. Murray was Assistant Professor of Egyptology at University College, London, until 1935. She took part in many excavations and wrote many books on archeology.

MYERS, FREDERICK WILLIAM HENRY (1843–1901)
A founder member and president of the Society for Psychical Research. Myers worked for 30 years as an inspector of schools in Cambridge. With Edmund Gurney and Frank Podmore, two other founders of the SPR, Myers collected stories of apparitions which were published as *Phantasms of the Living* (1886). Myers was one of the first people to use the word telepathy, and he believed this phenomenon was responsible for the appearance of many ghosts. He believed that a ghost was often a "crisis apparition" sent by a dying to a living person, but that it might not appear until after death because the percipient was too preoccupied with other matters to see it at the exact time. Myers' most important book, *Human Personality and Its Survival of Bodily Death*, outlines the theory that ordinary consciousness is but a fraction of the real ego, and that supernormal faculties are the channels of perception of the more important subliminal self. He thought that the powers of the subliminal self survive death. After investigating the Italian medium Eusapia Paladino, Myers became convinced that telekinesis and ectoplasm existed. In 1891–2 he wrote a paper for *Proceedings of the SPR* called: "On Alleged Movements of Objects without Contact, Occurring Not in the Presence of a Paid Medium." On the whole, however, he was not deeply interested in physical phenomena. After his death in 1901 two mediums, Mrs. Leonore Piper and Mrs. Willett, seemed to be in communication with Myers. They produced the so-called "cross-correspondences," scripts that were disjointed and meaningless as received separately, but that made sense when put together.

NAPIER, DR. JOHN (b. 1917)

British anthropologist and zoologist who has investigated stories of the Abominable Snowman and other giant creatures. In 1973 he wrote the book *Bigfoot* about the Yeti sightings in the Himalayas since 1832, and about the legendary Sasquatch, or Bigfoot, in North America. Dr. Napier was born near London, and went to London University. He was curator of the Primate Collection at the Smithsonian Institution in Washington, D.C., and is now Visiting Professor of Zoology at Birkbeck College, London. Before going to the United States Dr. Napier studied prehuman and early human fossils in South and East Africa. He worked with Dr. L. S. B. Leakey, the British anthropologist who discovered the remains of *homo habilis*, probably a two-million-year-old ancestor of man, in Tanzania. In the United States and Canada Dr. Napier investigated reports of the Bigfoot, and concluded: "I am convinced that the Sasquatch exists, but whether it is all that it is cracked up to be is another matter altogether. There must be *something* in northwest America that needs explaining, and that something leaves manlike footprints. The evidence I have adduced in favor of the reality of the Sasquatch is not hard evidence; few physicists, biologists, or chemists would accept it, but nevertheless it *is* evidence and cannot be ignored."

NOSTRADAMUS (1503–66)

Famous French clairvoyant. Nostradamus' real name was Michel de Nostredame, and he was born in St. Rémy, France. His grandfather was Jewish, but by the time Michel was 9, the family had converted to Christianity. Nostradamus studied Hebrew, Latin, Greek, mathematics, medicine, and astrology, and became a successful and popular doctor, working among victims of the plague which was then endemic in France. His interest in astrology, however, caused unfavorable comment in university circles. By the 1540s reports of Nostradamus' prophetic powers were circulating, and from 1551 he produced annual Almanacks and Prognostications. In 1555 Nostradamus published the first part of his major work *The Prophecies of Mr. Michael Nostradamus*. This work, completed in 1568, is generally known as *Centuries* because it is divided into 10 sections each containing 100 predictions. The *Centuries* were written in four-line rhymes of obscure and symbolic language so as not to offend the Church, and they lend themselves to many different interpretations. But enthusiasts claim that Nostradamus foresaw the death of King Charles I, the rise of Napoleon and Hitler, the atom bomb attacks on Hiroshima and Nagasaki, the abdication of King Edward VIII, and the deaths of John and Robert Kennedy. It is claimed that he also predicted a third world war, which will be started by China. Although the works of Nostradamus were condemned by the Papal Court and put on the Index in 1781, *Centuries* has remained continuously in print for 400 years. During World War II *Centuries* was used for propaganda purposes by both sides. The Nazis dropped copies of the predictions over France with texts translated so as to demoralize the people, and the Allies retaliated by scattering their own versions of Nostradamus' versus over German towns.

Below: a drawing of the medieval seer Nostradamus holding a marble tablet on which his prophecy about the French Revolution, more than 200 years after his lifetime, is inscribed. He is showing it to a peasant woman and her child.

OUSPENSKY, PETER DEMIANOVITCH (1878–1947)

Leading occultist often described as a disciple of Gurdjieff. Ouspensky was a Russian writer and lecturer who had been trained as a scientist. But he had become dissatisfied with modern values and plunged into a study of the occult, traveling extensively in the East. In 1915 Ouspensky met Gurdjieff and became one of his closest associates. Even after their break in 1924 because of a clash of personalities, Ouspensky continued to devote his life to teaching and expounding a system of thought like Gurdjieff's. From 1924 to 1940 he lived in London, and his lectures and study groups were attended by many well-known people. At the outbreak of World War II Ouspensky moved to New York where he continued writing and teaching. He returned to England in 1947 and died there the same year. In his *In Search of the Miraculous*, he gives a detailed account of his years with Gurdjieff and of Gurdjieff's ideas. Other important books were *Tertium Organum, A New Model of the Universe, The Fourth Way, and The Psychology of Man's Possible Evolution.*

PADRE PIO DA PIETRALCINI (1887–1968)

Italian Capuchin friar whose double was often seen in other places. Padre Pio spent most of his life at a monastery near Poggia, Italy, but was able to project his astral body to help people in trouble, notably during World Wars I and II. It is said that he received the stigmata in 1915, and he was credited with remarkable powers of clairvoyance and precognition. Pilgrims flocked to see him, but the Catholic Church had a reserved attitude toward him.

PALADINO, EUSAPIA (1854–1919)

Italian medium. She was born into a peasant family near Bari, and her mother died in childbirth. When she was 12 her father was murdered by brigands, and Eusapia Paladino became nursemaid to a family in Naples. This family was interested in Spiritualism. It is said that as a child Eusapia heard raps on the furniture, saw eyes glaring in the dark, and felt invisible hands strip the clothes off her bed. In 1872 Signor Damiani, an Italian psychic investigator, attended a seance in London. The famous spirit control, John King, manifested himself and spoke about a powerful medium in Naples who was his reincarnated daughter. King gave an address in Naples, where Signor Damiani found Eusapia Paladino. He had never heard of her before. John King was Eusapia Paladino's control, and he communicated through raps and spoke in Italian when she was in trance. It was said that she could materialize heads and hands, and occasionally complete bodies. She could levitate, increase and decrease her height, attract pieces of furniture toward her and cause them to levitate, and produce mysterious lights, noises, and scents. Eusapia Paladino occasionally was discovered in fraud; but after a thorough investigation in 1908 a committee of the Council of the Society for Psychical Research admitted that her powers were due to "some supernormal cause."

PARACELSUS (1493–1541)

Physician known for miraculous cures and as an alchemist.

Paracelsus was born near Zurich, Switzerland, the son of a physician. He traveled widely and studied many various fields of knowledge, but probably received his doctorate in 1515 at the famous medical school of Ferrara in northern Italy. Although his real name was Theophrastus Bombastus von Hohenheim, he adopted the pseudonym of Paracelsus, meaning "beyond Celsus," because it indicated that he was greater than Celsus, the famous doctor of Ancient Rome. Paracelsus was undoubtedly a gifted doctor, and many of his so-called miracle cures may have been due to the hypnotic power of his personality. He used his knowledge of alchemy in treating illnesses with mineral and chemical substances at a time when doctors were prescribing herbal remedies almost entirely, and his work led to the establishment of a school of medical chemistry. He was also responsible for the development of mystical alchemy, which emphasized the search for spiritual perfection over the search for the Philosopher's Stone to transmute metals to gold. Paracelsus was full of contradictions. He was brilliant and original, but his behavior was often vulgar and violent, needlessly antagonizing to his associates. When appointed Professor of Medicine at the University of Basel in 1524, one of his first acts was to publicly burn the works of Galen, Avicenna, and other honored physicians. After other such incidents, he was finally forced to leave the city and spent the rest of his life wandering from place to place, writing copiously. He died after rolling down a hill in a drunken stupor.

Above: Eusapia Paladino, a much-investigated Italian medium who produced a wide range of psychic phenomena. Although she was detected in fraud a few times, most investigators were convinced that she had genuine psychic powers.

PIPER, MRS. LEONORE E. (1857–1950)

Remarkable American medium who lived in Boston. Leonore Piper's first control was Phinuit, said to be the spirit of a French doctor. She would go into a deep trance and speak in a gruff male voice in a curious mixture of French, patois, and Yankee slang, sometimes swearing vulgarly. Phinuit, it is said, was able to relay messages from the dead that were accurate in the smallest details. Later Phinuit was replaced by George Pelham, Imperator, and other spirits. Mrs. Piper also practiced automatic writing, and some of her scripts form part of a set of writings known as the "cross-correspondences." These were produced at the beginning of the century by different mediums, though they apparently all came from F. W. H. Myers, a leading member of the Society for Psychical Research who had died in 1901, and his friends. The messages only make sense when put together. Some say that unconscious telepathy between the mediums may be the explanation. Dr. Richard Hodgson, another outstanding member of the British Society for Psychical Research, spent 15 years investigating Leonore Piper's activities as a medium, and even employed private detectives to follow her to make sure she did not gain her information by fraudulent means. He finally concluded that she was genuine, and that she was in some way in touch with the spirits of the dead.

PRICE, HARRY (1881–1948)

Well-known British psychic investigator and Britain's most famous ghost hunter of the 1920s and 1930s. He was a prominent member of the Society for Psychical Research to investigate psychic phenomena by scientific means. He was also an amateur magician, gaining the position of Honorary Vice-President of the Magician's Club in London. Price exposed many fraudulent mediums as well as supporting those he considered genuine. One of his most famous investigations was that of the Austrian medium Rudi Schneider, whom he at first championed and later accused of fraud. Price devised a ghost-hunting kit that included movie and still cameras, steel measuring-tape, portable telephone, flashlight, and first-aid kit. His reputation came under attack for his work at Borley Rectory, said to be the most haunted house in Britain. In a book called *The Haunting of Borley Rectory* (1956) by three members of the Society for Psychical Research, it was claimed that Price had suppressed some facts and exaggerated others about his investigation. However, even if these accusations are true, it cannot be denied that Price made a great contribution to psychic research. His best-known books were *Rudi Schneider: a Scientific Examination of his Mediumship* (1930), *Fifty Years of Psychical Research* (1939), and *The Most Haunted House in England* (1940). At his death he left thousands of books on psychical research to London University, which have been preserved in the Harry Price Library.

PRINCE, REVEREND HENRY JAMES (1811–99)
English clergyman who believed he was the Holy Ghost personified, and who founded the Agapemonite cult. Ordained in the Church of England in 1840, Prince became a curate in Somerset. He was a brilliant orator who attracted many people from surrounding parishes to hear him. His rector, Reverend Starky believed he had the voice of God. Banned from preaching in Anglican churches in 1841, Prince began holding services in barns. He was accompanied by his disciple Starky. In 1849 Prince and Starky opened Agapemone, the Abode of Love, in a spacious mansion near Spaxton, Somerset. Money poured in from rich admirers, and a wave of fanaticism swept the area. Letters were addressed to Prince as "Our Holy Lord at Spaxton." The cult even drew several prominent members of the Salvation Army. Agapemone soon got a reputation for excessive drinking and sexual license, however.

PUHARICH, DR. ANDRIJA (b. 1918)
American neurologist and psychic researcher. Born in Chicago, Puharich graduated from the Northwestern University Medical School in 1947, and worked at Permanente Hospital in California. His wide interest in psychical phenomena arose out of an academic curiosity about telepathy. He set up his own laboratory for the study of ESP and parapsychology in which his subjects included the medium Eileen Garrett and the psychometrist Peter Hurkos. In 1960 Dr. Puharich led an expedition to Oaxaca, Mexico, to study the sacred mushroom rite of the Chatino Indians, and between 1963 and 1968 he investigated the Brazilian psychic surgeon José Arigó. While in Brazil, Puharich claimed to have seen flying saucers, which he photographed. In 1971 Puharich visited Uri Geller in Israel, and decided that Geller is a divine messenger from "super beings" who have been watching the earth for thousands of years.

RASPUTIN, GRIGORI YEFIMOVICH (about 1870–1916)

Russian faith healer who had great influence on the royal family. Born of peasant stock in Pokrovskoe, Siberia, Rasputin seemed from an early age to have believed that he had a special mission in life. He married in 1890, and after the death of his baby son turned more and more to religion. After several years he had a vision of the Holy Virgin and decided to make a pilgrimage to Mount Athos in Greece. When he returned two years later he had developed a strange personal magnetism that attracted many followers. Converting a barn into a temple, he soon gained a reputation as a holy man and healer. After a time he traveled to the capital of St. Petersburg, where he was taken up by the aristocracy and introduced to the czar. The czar's small son suffered from hemophilia, and after a fall in 1907, began to hemorrhage internally. His life was despaired of, but Rasputin saved him within a few minutes of seeing and talking to him. From then on Rasputin was extremely influential at court, close to both the czar and the czarina. Many believed that he was responsible for the czar's reactionary policies. In December 1916 he was lured into a cellar, poisoned, shot, and beaten with an iron bar—but survived. Finally he was dropped through a hole in the ice of the Neva River, and drowned.

RAUDIVE, DR. KONSTANTIN (1909–74)

Latvian psychologist who taped about 100,000 voice samples that he believed emanated from the dead. In the 1960s Dr. Raudive worked on the so-called "voice phenomena" experiments with Swedish film producer Friedrich Jurgenson and a group of German scientists. He published his research in the book *Breakthrough—Amazing Experiment in Electronic Communication with the Dead*, which appeared in an English version

Below: Rasputin, Russian mystic and faith healer, pictured with a group of aristocratic admirers. Through successful treatment of the czar's sickly child, Rasputin became a power in the royal court.

Above: Professor J. B. Rhine, American parapsychologist who pioneered modern psychical research, mainly at Duke University.

in 1971. Before allowing publication of the book in England, publisher Sir Robert Mayer insisted that further experiments be carried out and checked by independent scientists and electronic engineers. Controlled tests were made by the two chief engineers of Pye Ltd., and over 200 voices manifested themselves during a 20 minute recording. One voice seemed to be that of the great pianist Artur Schnabel, who had been a friend of Sir Robert Mayer. Often a taped message is in a mixture of several languages.

REICH, WILHELM (1897–1957)

Psychoanalyst who developed a theory of the existence of orgone energy, a life force that he believed permeates the universe. Dr. Reich studied medicine at Vienna University, and practiced Freudian psychoanalysis for a time. His work convinced him that sexual repression leads people to build up a shell to cover weakness and anxiety, which may express itself in tension and muscular rigidity and lead to neurosis. One of his most controversial ideas in treatment was that a satisfactory sexual orgasm will dispel this neurosis. Slowly he began to equate sexual energy with the life force that he called orgone energy. He claimed to have observed bions, units of orgone energy, through a microscope. It is not too clear what Reich meant by orgone energy, but he apparently believed that it could be extracted from the atmosphere and used for treating mental and physical illnesses. Reich built wood and metal "orgone energy accumulators," large upright boxes big enough for a person to sit in. He moved to the United States and established a research and teaching center in Maine. When he started to sell his books and orgone accumulators, the U.S. Food and Drug Administration obtained an injunction against Reich, accusing him of distributing fraudulent devices. Reich disregarded the injunction of 1950 and was sent to prison for contempt of court. He died in jail. Reich's books include: *The Function of the Orgasm, Contact with Space,* and *The Sexual Revolution.* Since his death Reich has become a cult figure, admired both as a champion of sexual freedom, and as an "unconscious magician" who rediscovered the "astral light" of Paracelsus, Lévi, and Aleister Crowley.

RHINE, PROFESSOR J. B. (b. 1895)

American pioneer of experimental research in parapsychology. In 1927 he resigned a teaching post at West Virginia University to study psychical research under the famous psychologist Professor William McDougall at Duke University, North Carolina. In 1930 Rhine became Director of the Parapsychology Laboratory at Duke University, and later Executive Director of the Foundation for Research on the Nature of Man. Professor Rhine preferred the term "parapsychology" to "psychic research" because he thought it would be more acceptable to modern scientists. He tested telepathy, clairvoyance, precognition, and psychokinesis in strictly controlled laboratory conditions, but was also concerned with psychic phenomena in everyday life and with religious matters. He believed that the question of survival after death should be investigated by scientific methods. Professor Rhine tested telepathy using a pack of 25 specially designed cards. In one of his tests, Rhine's assistants tried to transmit messages to people in the laboratory, sometimes from miles away. Rhine found that certain people nearly always got a higher percentage of right guesses than the statistical possibility of one in five. When given sedative drugs, the high guessers were less successful, but when given stimulants such as coffee, their accuracy improved. Professor Rhine got similar results in his tests with dice. In a series of experiments lasting eight years he showed that the mind can influence the fall of the dice, and that a person's psychic powers are greatest when he or she is enthusiastic and alert, but decline when tired and bored. Rhine's books include: *Extrasensory Perception* (1934), *New Frontiers of the Mind* (1937), *Parapsychology: Frontier Science of the Mind* (1957), and *Extrasensory Perception after 60 Years* (1966).

RICHET, CHARLES (1850–1935)

Eminent French physiologist and outstanding psychical researcher. He was Professor of Physiology at the Faculty of Medicine in Paris and winner of the Nobel prize in 1915. While still a student he established that hypnotism was a physiological phenomenon, not due to magnetic fluids as was widely believed. He experimented with subjects who were able to reproduce drawings contained in sealed envelopes, without having seen them, and came to the conclusion that a faculty of cognition exists outside our normal range of knowledge. In 1895 he became President of the Society for Psychical Research. He investigated many famous mediums including Eusapia Paladino and Rudi Schneider, and his work with Eva C in Algeria convinced him of the reality of materializations. He coined the term "ectoplasm" for the strange substances that mediums frequently produced. He was a cautious and meticulous investigator and anxious that other scientists should approach the problem of psychic phenomena with an open mind. His most important book in this field was probably *Thirty Years of Psychical Research*, published in English in 1923.

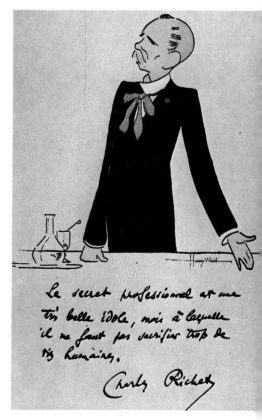

Above: a 1908 cartoon making fun of Dr. Charles Richet, a famous French physiologist, for his interest in psychical phenomena.

Below: Richet, who was one of Eusapia Paladino's supporters, shown with other researchers taking wax molds of spirit hands.

Right: Rudi Schneider, Austrian medium especially known for materializations, being tested by the colorful English psychical investigator Harry Price. A great controversy arose when Price accused the young medium of fraud on evidence that did not satisfy his fellow psychical researchers.

SCHNEIDER, WILLI (b. 1903) and RUDI (1908–57)

Austrian brothers who were both mediums. They were born in Braunau, the sons of a linotype compositor. Willi's psychic powers were discovered when he was 16 when he began to do automatic writing. One day, in answer to the question: "Who is there?" the pencil wrote: "Olga, Lola Montez." Lola Montez was the mistress of King Ludwig I of Bavaria and had died in New York in 1861. She became Willi's spirit control. Willi was studied by the well-known psychic researcher Baron von Schrenck Notzing, and between 1921 and 1922 many scientists claimed to have witnessed his ability to make objects move by will power and to produce ectoplasm. Willi's powers soon waned, and his control transferred to his brother Rudi. Rudi held his first independent seances in Braunau in 1919, when materialization of a tiny hand was seen. His other phenomena included movement of objects, levitation, and the ringing of bells. Rudi was investigated in London in 1929 and 1932 by Harry Price, the founder and director of the National Laboratory of Psychical Research, and by Dr. Eugene Osty, a well-known psychical researcher, in Paris in 1930 and 1931. On one occasion Dr. Osty set up an infrared system that would automatically sound bells and take pictures if any arm or device approached the table on which the objects to be moved were placed. The alarm bell went off several times when Olga said she was "going into a ray," but photographs showed that the infrared rays had not been interrupted by anything physical. By 1932 Rudi's psychic abilities appeared to be fading, and 18 out of 28 seances held at Harry Price's National Laboratory of Psychical Research in London were negative. Moreover, Price believed that he had detected him in fraud, an accusation that aroused a great deal of controversy among psychic investigators.

SEABROOK, WILLIAM (1886–1945)

American traveler and author who wrote about witchcraft and kindred subjects. Seabrook was born in Westminster, Maryland, and contributed to many leading American newspapers and magazines including the *New York Times*. From 1924 on he spent most of his time traveling. He lived as a member of a Bedouin tribe with the Druses in Arabia; stayed at a whirling dervish monastery in Tripoli and with Zezidee devil worshippers in Kurdistan; spent a year with voodoo worshippers in Haiti; and

visited West Africa. During his time in Haiti Seabrook was initiated into voodoo ritual, and described his meeting with a zombie. He also wrote about a West African clerk, Tei, who had been caught wearing a panther skin with iron claws after murdering a girl on a jungle path. Tei believed that he really became a panther when dressed in the skin. Seabrook's books include: *The White Monk of Timbuctoo* (1934), *Witchcraft* (1940), and an autobiography, *No Hiding Place* (1942).

SERIOS, TED (b. 1918)
American "thought photographer." Serios was born in Kansas City, Missouri, the son of Greek café owner. In 1963 Serios impressed Dr. Jule Eisenbud, a psychiatrist, with his ability to produce "thought photographs." Serios would stare down a small paper tube, which he called a "gismo," into the lens of a camera. An assistant flicked the shutter, and the pictures taken were of images in his mind. On one occasion, for example, Serios produced a picture of the clock tower of Westminster Abbey, which he had seen in a photograph the day before. He has been carefully tested for fraud, but so far there has been no proof that he is not genuine.

SIDGWICK, PROFESSOR HENRY (1838–1900)
First President of the Society for Psychical Research in England. Sidgwick was Professor of Moral Philosophy at Cambridge University, and was once described as "the most incorrigibly and exasperatingly critical and skeptical mind in England." On becoming President of the SPR in 1882 he said: "I say it is a scandal that the dispute as to the reality of these [psychic] phenomena should still be going on, that so many competent witnesses have declared their belief in them . . . and yet the educated world, as a body, should still be simply in an attitude of incredulity." Professor Sidgwick took part in many psychic investigations. He was impressed by the phenomena produced by Eusapia Paladino, the Italian medium. He contributed many important studies to the *Proceedings* of the SPR. After his death several mediums claimed to have received communications from him.

SILVA, EDIVALDO OLIVEIRA (about 1930–74)
Brazilian Spiritist healer and psychic surgeon. Edivaldo was a secondary school teacher and professional taxidermist. He discovered his healing powers by accident in 1962 after visiting a sick neighbor. Like most psychic surgeons, Edivaldo performed operations on the "subtle" rather than the physical body. He went into trance, spoke in the voices of his spirit guides, and moved his hands about in the air above the injury or sick tissue. Later he had no conscious memory of performing the operations. According to Guy Playfair, author of *The Flying Cow*, the surgery was invisible to onlookers, but the patients undoubtedly felt something. In his 12-year career Edivaldo treated about 65,000 people and performed at least 10,000 operations. All that time he was studying medicine and law, and hoped to qualify as a doctor so that he could do his healing work without danger of prosecution for illegal practice. However, he died in a road accident after a collision with a truck in 1974.

SOAL, DR. SAMUEL G. (1889–1975)

Mathematician and President of the Society for Psychical Research from 1949 to 1951. Soal was skeptical about Professor J. B. Rhine's early telepathy experiments at Duke University in North Carolina, and decided to run a series of card tests of his own in London. By 1939 he had made 120,000 trials with 140 different people, but found no confirmatory evidence of telepathy. However, he followed a suggestion to test the "displacement effect," that is, for right guesses just before or just after the target card. Soal found that professional photographer Basil Shackleton guessed the card following the target card correctly on 1101 out of 3789 occasions. Soal attributed this power either to precognition or the psychic ability to look into the unturned cards. Dr. Soal also took part in experiments with stage telepathist Frederick Marion at London University, at the end of which he wrote a 96-page report, "Preliminary Studies of a Vaudeville Telepathist." His books include *Modern Experiments in Telepathy* (1954), with F. Bateman, and *The Mind Readers* (1959), with H. T. Bowden.

SOUTHCOTT, JOANNA (1750–1814)

English cult figure. She believed she was the Bride of Christ and the Second Eve sent to redeem mankind, and she gained many followers who also believed this. Born into a family of poor farmers, Joanna Southcott did an exorcism for a dying man when still in her teens. She began to hear a supernatural voice uttering prophecies when she was in her forties. In 1801 Thomas B. Foley, rector in Old Swinford, conducted a test of her gifts and was convinced that she had the power of prophecy. Further tests in 1803 and 1804 increased her fame. Joanna Southcott saw references to herself as the Second Eve in the Book of Revelation. In her mid-sixties she believed that she was going to give birth to Shiloh, the Second Messiah promised in Revelation. According to a biographer, several doctors examined her and confirmed that she was pregnant. However, the promised date of the miraculous birth—October 19, 1814—came and went, and a new date was set for December 24. On December 27 Joanna Southcott died. An autopsy revealed a swollen condition of the womb. She had bombarded bishops, peers, and members of the House of Commons with letters, and had prepared a sealed box containing her revelations, which she said was to be opened by bishops after her death. It was reported that the Archbishop of Canterbury opened the box in 1927, but it contained nothing of importance. The Panacea Society in England claims it still has the sealed box of her writings.

SPARE, AUSTIN OSMAN (1886–1956)

English artist who devoted his life to magic. Spare was born in London, the son of a policeman. He studied at the Royal College of Art, where his talent was quickly recognized. The way seemed open for a successful career, but Spare deliberately made a choice to pursue his interest in the occult. As a child he had formed a close friendship with an old woman who claimed to be a witch, and she had taught him how to travel to other planes of existence, and how to invoke spirits and elementals. Spare

Right: *Flame, Fugue, and Flesh,* a pastel drawing of 1954 by the English artist and magician Austin Spare. Magic came first with him, and he used his art to express his occult experiences rather than to build a career.

pursued and developed her ideas and used his art to illustrate the strange spirit worlds he claimed to have explored. In *The Book of Pleasure* (1913), he describes how superhuman powers can be called upon from deep layers of the subconscious. In *The Focus of Life* (1921), Spare stressed the importance of sex in magic. From 1927 till his death he lived as a semi-recluse in London, holding occasional local exhibitions of his work.

SPENCE, LEWIS (1874–1955)

Scottish poet and occultist who wrote books about the lost continents of Atlantis and Lemuria. Born near Dundee, Scotland, Spence was educated at Edinburgh University and studied dentistry. Later he became a journalist, working as a copy editor on the *Scotsman* and the *British Weekly*. He wrote several volumes of verse in Scottish dialect, which had a major influence on the revival of Scottish literature. Spence was one of the founders of the Scottish National Party in 1929. After studying the early civilizations of Mexico and Central America, he published *The Civilisation of Ancient Mexico* (1911), *Myths of Mexico and Peru* (1913) and *The Gods of Mexico* (1923). Branching out into magic and the occult, Spence wrote *Encyclopaedia of Occultism* (1920), *The Magic Arts of Celtic Britain* (1945), and *The History and Origins of Druidism* (1950). Spence was the Chosen Chief of Edward Kenealy's Druid Order, and was responsible for the introduction of magical practices into the Druid Order. In 1924 he wrote a major work, *The Problem of Atlantis*, in which he claimed that a great continent formerly occupied most of the North Atlantic region and part of the southern basin. Toward the end of the Miocene period 10 to 25 million years ago, he said, it began to break up following volcanic eruptions. Two large insular masses were formed, linked by smaller islands. One was Atlantis near the entrance to the Mediterranean; the other was Antillia in the West Indies region. Spence believed that Atlantis disappeared slowly, and he did not claim, like other writers, that Atlantis was the source of all civilization. He did, however, think that refugees from Atlantis and Antillia founded the Egyptian, Cretan, and Mayan civilizations. He also believed there was an equally strong case for the former existence of Lemuria, about which he wrote in *The Problem of Lemuria* (1933). His other books on the subject of Atlantis include *Atlantis in America* (1925), *The History of Atlantis* (1926), *The Occult Sciences in Atlantis* and *Will Europe Follow Atlantis?* (1942).

STEINER, DR. RUDOLF (1861–1925)

Austrian educator and writer who broke away from the Theosophists to form his own Anthroposophical Society. Steiner was born in Kraljevic, then in Austro-Hungary, the son of a railroad employee. In 1879 the family moved to Vienna, where Steiner came under the influence of the Theosophists. He worked at the Goethe Archive in Weimar from 1890, editing Goethe's scientific works, and gaining a Ph.D. degree. In 1897 he went to Berlin and became editor of the *Magazin für Literatur* (Literary Magazine). Steiner became disillusioned with certain aspects of the Theosophical Society and formed his own group. In 1906 he accepted a charter from an occult organization, the OTO or Order of the Temple of the Orient, which was accused of practicing sexual magic. Later he developed his own form of Rosicrucianism, mingling the Theosophist theory of reincarnation with European occultism, some of Goethe's philosophical ideas, and his own brand of Christianity. The new movement was known as Anthroposophy, or "Man-Wisdom," and was intended to provide the solution to society's artistic, political, and social problems. Steiner claimed he had clairvoyant faculties which he used to look into the past and write *Cosmic Memory*. *Atlantis and Lemuria*. He derived his knowledge from the "Akasha Chronicle"—a spiritual record of the past known only to the initiated. According to Steiner, the Atlanteans and Lemurians were unable to reason but had extraordinary memories, and used the magic power of words to heal the sick and tame wild animals. Steiner was also one of the pioneers of progressive education after World War I. In the 1960s there were still over 70 schools run on Anthroposophical lines in different parts of the world. His many books include: *Occult Science: an Outline*, *Christianity as Mystical Fact*, *Knowledge of the Higher Worlds and its Attainments*, and *Theosophy of the Rosicrucians*.

STOKER, BRAM (1847–1912)

Irish novelist who wrote *Dracula*. Stoker was an invalid as a child, but he became a champion athlete during his years at Trinity College, Dublin. For 10 years he worked in the Irish Civil Service, wrote theater reviews for the *Dublin Mail*, and edited the *Irish Echo*. Then on the invitation of Henry Irving, the famous actor-manager, he became business manager of the Lyceum Theater in London. In the 1870s Stoker began writing horror stories, including *The Burial of the Rats* and *The Squaw*. In 1897 he published *Dracula*, which was an immediate success and appeared in dramatized form as *Dracula or the Un-Dead* at the Lyceum Theater only a few days after publication of the novel. Stoker said that his book was inspired by a nightmare. He dreamed of a vampire rising from the grave one night after he had eaten too much crab for supper. He set the story of Dracula in Rumania, the legendary home of vampires, and his Count Dracula—with aquiline face, high-bridged thin nose, arched nostrils, and long black cloak—has come to typify the idea of a vampire. The story of Dracula has been used in many films, and helped the careers of several actors. Stoker wrote other stories including *The Lair of the White Worm*, which was about a monster that hid in a deep well for thousands of years, and was able to project itself in the form of a woman in white with a low voice and long flexible hands. A sequel to *Dracula* called *Dracula's Guest* appeared two years after Stoker's death.

SUBUH, PAK (b. 1901)

Indonesian mystic who founded the Subud movement. Pak Subuh's real name is Mohammed Subuh Sumojadiwidjojo. As a child he had clairvoyant powers. In 1925, when he was working as a clerk in the municipal treasurer's office in Semarang, Java, he had an experience that changed his life. While walking home one evening a globe of light descended from the sky and entered

Above: Bram Stoker, author of the popular horror tale *Dracula*. His spine-chilling book about the Rumanian count who was a vampire started a continuing series of films and stories on vampirism.

Above: Ingo Swann, artist and psychic, cooperates in many tests like this one on out-of-the-body experiences. He is able consciously to control his psychic powers.

his body through the top of his head. Subuh felt purified and in possession of a new power. He had many other spiritual experiences, and by the age of 33 was ready to pass on his knowledge of God. His followers increased until today there are Subud groups in nearly every country of the non-communist world. Initiation takes place through a process known as "opening." The initiate stands for about half an hour with his "openers" and allows the Life Force to enter him. Subuh followers attend half-hour sessions of *latihan* (Indonesian for "exercise") two or three times a week, and these are intended to increase the Life Force. One Subud practitioner described the *latihan* experience as "a sort of resurrection." Other people have felt nothing at all during *latihan*, and one or two, it is claimed, have been made mentally ill.

SWANN, INGO (b.1933)

Artist and astral projector. He was born in Colorado and studied art and biology. In 1958 he moved to New York to work with the United Nations and to begin his career as an artist. He started painting auras around objects, and the strange arrangement of bubbles and energy flares that he saw with the naked eye were later confirmed through Kirlian photography. Swann had experienced out-of-the-body projection ever since he had been a small child, and he willingly cooperated in out-of-the-body vision experiments with the American Society for Psychical Research. He also took part in a series of experiments at the City College of New York in which he was able to affect the

temperature of scientific apparatus from a distance, and participated in a series of strictly controlled experiments at Stanford Research Institute. Many of these are described in his book *To Kiss the Earth Goodbye*, published in 1975.

Above: *Galaxy Forward*, **a work of 1973 by Swann in oil and aluminum on canvas. The aim is to make the viewer "experience psychic sensations of speed and motion."**

SWEDENBORG, EMANUEL (1688–1722)

Swedish philosopher, engineer, and mystic. Born in Stockholm, the second son of a highly educated and deeply religious Lutheran bishop, Swedenborg studied mathematics and engineering, and then traveled abroad to gain wider experience. His brilliant reputation was already well-established when in 1716 he was appointed Assessor to the Swedish Board of Mines. In 1734 he published his extremely important work *Opera Philosophica et Mineralia* on the formation of the planets. He followed this with other major books on anatomy, geology, and mineralogy, and on the relationship between the soul and the body. By 1745, with his publication of *Worship and the Love of God*, he had turned his attention totally to religion. He believed he was in direct communication with heavenly spirits, and his books recorded his conversations. However, even though they were based firmly on his mystical experiences, they were also serious and scholarly works of difficult reading. He also had clairvoyant powers, at one time describing a fire that had just broken out in Stockholm while having dinner 250 miles away. The Church of the New Jerusalem, or the Swedenborgian Church, was founded after his death, and many of his ideas influenced the Spiritualist movement that developed in the 1850s.

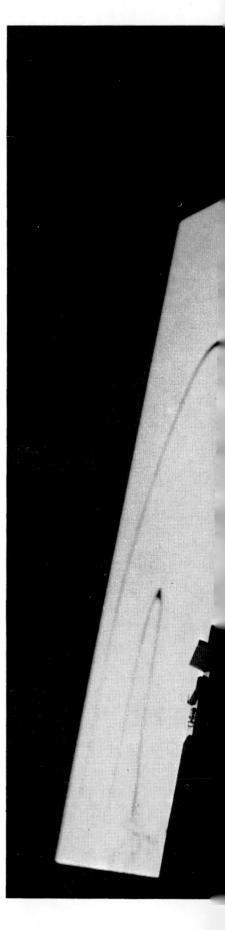

Right: Erich von Däniken, author of sensational best-selling books about space people as the possible ancestors of humans, shown lecturing in the United States.

VALLÉE, DR. JACQUES (b. 1939)

French computer expert who has investigated and written about sightings of flying saucers. Dr. Vallée was born in Pontoise, France, and educated at the Sorbonne and Lille Universities. He worked for the French Committee on Space Studies in Paris in 1961 and 1962, and then became a Research Associate at the Macdonald Observatory in Fort Davis, Texas, taking part in the NASA Mars Map Project as a computer consultant. In recent years he has worked as a mathematician-analyst at Northwestern University. Vallée wrote *Anatomy of a Phenomenon: UFOs in Space* (1965); *Challenge to Science: the UFO Enigma*, with his wife Janine (1966), and *Passport to Magonia* (1969), a book about flying saucers and ancient folklore. Dr. Vallée has conducted research into flying saucers at the Center for UFO Studies in America with Dr. J. Allen Hynek, a former astronomical consultant to the United States Air Force who did not approve of the way United States officials dismissed many inexplicable UFO sightings.

VASILIEV, DR. LEONID (1891–1966)

Chairman of Physiology at Leningrad University and pioneer in psychic research in the Soviet Union. In 1960 Vasiliev told a meeting of top Soviet scientists that it was essential to research ESP because the American Navy was testing whether telepathy could be used on atomic submarines. He said: "The discovery of the energy underlying ESP will be equivalent to the discovery of atomic energy." A year later Vasiliev became head of a special Parapsychology Laboratory at Leningrad University. He began experimenting with ESP in the 1930s, probably on orders from Stalin, and described in *Experiments in Mental Suggestion* (1962) how he ran hundreds of tests trying to "think" people into action. For example, he tried to make others cross their legs or raise their hands by his thought power. They responded to the mental suggestions too frequently for coincidence. One of the most spectacular tests done by Vasiliev was with a subject in a room that excluded electromagnetic radiation, thus eliminating any possible physical communication as a medium of exchange in telepathy. Many of the early Soviet experiments were in telepathic hypnotism with subjects hundreds of miles away. Dr. Vasiliev also did experiments with Nelya Mikhailova, the psychic whose gifts include "seeing" colors with her fingers.

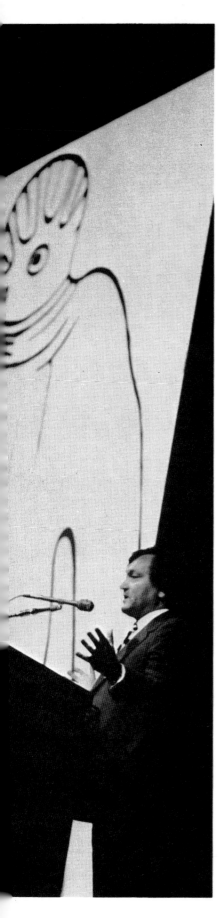

VELIKOVSKY, DR. IMMANUEL (b. 1895)

Russian-born psychoanalyst and scholar who caused a sensation with his book *Worlds in Collision*, which suggested that cosmic forces in the past may have influenced the development of human history. Velikovsky was born in Vitebsk, and studied natural sciences and medicine at Moscow University and other European institutions. He practiced as a psychoanalyst between 1924 and 1939, then moved to the United States where he now lives in Princeton. Dr. Velikovsky believes that an enormous comet swept close to the earth on several occasions in the distant past, and finally became the planet Venus. He claims that the action of this comet caused the parting of the waters of the Red Sea, made the walls of Jericho collapse, and led to the disappearance of Atlantis. Dr. Velikovsky suggests that land and sea repeatedly changed places during cosmic cataclysms, that the animal kingdom and human race were submerged, and that increased radioactivity led to the spontaneous emergence of new species following each global catastrophe. *Worlds in Collision* (1950) created such a storm that orthodox scientists tried to stop its publication. Dr. Velikovsky has also written *Ages in Chaos* (1952), and *Earth in Upheaval* (1955). His scholarship was defended by no less a scientist than Albert Einstein.

VON DÄNIKEN, ERICH (b. 1935)

Swiss author who writes that astronauts visiting Earth from another solar system in ancient times were the forefathers of mankind. Von Däniken was born in Zofingen, Switzerland, and was brought up as a Roman Catholic. He attended St. Michel College in Fribourg, and then worked as a hotelier. From an early age Von Däniken's main interest was to discover the truth about human evolution. He studied the biblical prophets, and believed that Ezekiel's account of "fiery chariots" was a description of spaceships that had visited the Earth. He read ancient Indian and Tibetan scripts, visited stone relics in South America, Egypt, Great Britain, and Easter Island, and examined rock drawings in North Africa and other countries. Von Däniken claimed that in all these places he found evidence that the ancient myths about gods coming from the skies were based on fact. He believed, for example, that the geometric patterns on a strip of land in Nazca, Peru were the work of inhabitants of another planet who made an airfield there thousands of years ago. In the Tassili mountains of Algeria, he found rock drawings of men who, according to Von Däniken, were wearing spacesuits with steering gear on their shoulders and antennas on their helmets. In his book *Chariots of the Gods* (1969) Von Däniken concluded that the gods who visited from outer space artificially fertilized the females of the apelike species that then inhabited the earth, and after generations of cross-breeding produced humans. Von Däniken has also written *Return to the Stars* (1970), *The Gold of the Gods* (1972), *In Search of Ancient Gods* (1973), and *Miracles of the Gods* (1975). Worldwide sales of his books approach 30 million. Von Däniken has been strongly criticized by scholars who say that not only does he distort archeological evidence, but also that he ignores any facts which tend to cast doubt on or disprove his theories.

WATKINS, ALFRED (about 1855–1935)

English merchant and amateur archeologist who developed the theory of "ley lines," supposed lines of force linking ancient mounds, stones, crossroads, churches, prehistoric sites, and holy wells. In the 1920s when riding across the Herefordshire hills where he lived, Watkins looked down and saw in a vision a vast network of straight tracks. He later called these ley lines. Checking an Ordnance Survey map he found that ancient sites throughout the countryside were connected by absolutely straight lines, as he had seen them. Watkins was wary of the occult although he had had a close telepathic relationship with his sister. However, he wrote in *The Old Straight Track* (1925): "I feel that the ley-man, astronomer-priest, druid, bard, wizard, witch, palmer and hermit were all more or less linked by one thread of ancient knowledge and power."

WESTCOTT, DR. WILLIAM WYNN (1848–1925)

A London coroner who was also an occultist. He was one of the founders of the Order of the Golden Dawn, and also a leading member of the Rosicrucian Society in England. In 1887 Westcott received a manuscript written in cipher, which had allegedly been found on a secondhand bookstall by a middle-aged clergyman two years earlier. When deciphered the manuscript revealed magic rituals and, according to Westcott, the name of a German magical order. Westcott claimed that he wrote to the German group and was given permission to form a society called The Isis-Urania Temple of the Golden Dawn in London in 1888, but it seems from other evidence that this may have been a fabrication. Nonetheless, he formed the society with co-founders Dr. William Woodman, a retired doctor who had studied the Cabala in Hebrew, and Samuel Liddell McGregor Mathers. Before long the Golden Dawn had branches in other parts of England, and its members included such prominent people as the poet W. B. Yeats. Westcott became administrator of the Golden Dawn, but was later forced to resign from it by his employers as a condition of remaining a public servant.

Right: early photograph of members of the Rosicrucian Society in England showing Dr. William Wynn Westcott in the foreground. Westcott was a leading occultist of his period, one of the three founders of a well-known society for the study of magic known as the Order of the Golden Dawn.

Series Index

The aim of this index is to provide a quick easy-to-use reference to all the 19 volumes of the series. Each page reference in the index is preceded by initials in heavy black type. These initials refer to the volume in which the page reference will be found. The abbreviations are explained in a code key which has been repeated through the index. Page numbers in italics refer to captions.

Code Key

all in YAR

Alchemy

Alexander the Great

apparitions

Code Key

See pp. 66-67 for call nos.

*Astrology of
Personality*

Aztecs

Code Key

"Bermuda Triangle"

See pp. 66-67 for call nos.

Bernheim, Hippolyte

Boehme, Jakob

Code Key

AA: Alchemy, the Ancient Science

AL: Atlantis and the Lost Lands

CI: The Cosmic Influence

DW: Dream Worlds

EM: Enigmas and Mysteries

GP: Ghosts and Poltergeists

HM: Healing Without Medicine

MB: Minds Without Boundaries

MM: Monsters and Mythic Beasts

bogeys

bogeys, **VZ** 91–2

bokor (sorcerer), of voodoo, **VZ** 74

bone-setters, *see* osteopathy

Bonnington, Chris, on the Yeti, **MM** 113

Book of Change, The, see I Ching

book test, of Sir William Barrett, **SS** 140–1

books in stone, **MW** 124–40

Borley Rectory, psychic phenomena investigated by Harry Price, **GP** 109–13

Boshier, Adrian, witch doctor, on parapsychology, **MB** 11, *12*, 13

Boullan, Joseph Antoine, satanist, **WW** 109–10

Bourne, J., and the Yeti, **MM** *129*

Bovis, pyramidologist, **WA** 66

Bowes-Lyon, most haunted family in Britain, **GP** *76*, *77*, 78–80

Boyle, Robert, founder member of the Royal Society, **AA** 101–2

Bozo, the Minnesota Iceman, **MM** 127, *127*

Bradley, Dennis, writer on direct spirit voice contact, **SS** 104

Brahman, **MP** 45, **SS** 33

Braid, Dr. James, inventor of term "hypnotism," **HM** *105*, 107

brain function: during sleep, **DW** 94, 96–7; influence on philosophies of East and West, **WA** 8, 10

Bran Castle, in vampire tourism, **VZ** *20*

Brasseur de Bourbourg, Abbé Charles-Etienne, scholar, on Mayan alphabet, **AL** 68

Brazil: lost cities of, **AL** 54; religions of, **WA** 102–3; Spiritualism in, **SS** *116–17*, 117–20, *118*; "world's most psychic country," **HM** 94

Breakthrough, (by Konstantin Raudive), **SS** 94

breathing: and the spirit, **MP** 45; in yoga, **MP** *106*, **WA** 44, 47

Bredon Hill, Gloucestershire, site of ancient religious rites, **EM** *71*, 71–2

Brick, Hans, animal trainer, telepathy of, **MP** 18–19

Bridge of Parting, of ancient Persian belief, **SS** 30

bridges, between levels of the universe, **EM** 142

Brinvilliers, Marquise de, and the poison scandals of Louis XIV, **WW** *102*

British Association for the Advancement of Science, Sir William Crookes' address to, **SS** 60

British Premonitions Bureau, **DW** 114

British Society for Music Therapy, **HM** 125

Britten, Emma Hardinge, medium, **SS** 20–1, *20*, 116

Brocken: black magic at, investigated by Harry Price, **MB** 62, 64–6; explanation of specter, **GP** *122*, *124*

bronchitis, healed by hypnosis, **HM** *113*

Brontë, Emily, and the haunting of the Toby Jug, **GP** 119

Brontosaurus, **MM** *93*

Brown, Dr. Frank A: on "biological clocks," **CI** 32–4; on theory of astrology, **CI** 45

Brown, Professor J. MacMillan, on Easter Island, **AL** 71–2

Brown, John, medium to Queen Victoria, **SS** 20–1, *21*

Brown, Mrs. Rosemary, medium, receiver of automatic music writing, **SS** 122–3, *124–5*

brownies, **VZ** 90

Browning, Robert, **HM** *133*

brutality, attraction of, **VZ** *136*, 138

Bryant, E. A., contact with space visitors, **VO** 97

Buckland, Raymond, witch, **WW** 20

Buckland, Raymond

See pp. 66–67 for call nos.

Buddha

Carnarvon, Earl of

Code Key

AA : Alchemy, the Ancient Science

AL : Atlantis and the Lost Lands

CI : The Cosmic Influence

DW : Dream Worlds

EM : Enigmas and Mysteries

GP : Ghosts and Poltergeists

HM : Healing Without Medicine

MB : Minds Without Boundaries

MM : Monsters and Mythic Beasts

Carrington, Dr Hereward

Charcot, Jean Martin

see pp. 66–67 for call nos.

Chariots of the Gods

coaches, phantom

Code Key

Cobb, John

Cooper, Mrs Blanche

See pp. 66 · 67 for call nos.

Corbett, Jim

Crowley, Aleister

Code Key

de Landa, Diego

de Rais, Gilles

disappearance

Code Key

disaster, global

dreams

see pp. 66-67 for call nos.

dreams (continued)

dying, process of

Code Key

Elisha

See pp. 66-67 for call nos.

Code Key

Fludd, Robert

see pp. 66–67 for call nos.

fluid, psychic

Frankenstein

Code Key

AA: Alchemy, the Ancient Science

AL: Atlantis and the Lost Lands

CI: The Cosmic Influence

DW: Dream Worlds

EM: Enigmas and Mysteries

GP: Ghosts and Poltergeists

HM: Healing Without Medicine

MB: Minds Without Boundaries

MM: Monsters and Mythic Beasts

fraud

Geller, Uri

see also:
GELLER PHENOMENON
133.8 W699
(part of series, but not
included in Code Key)

Code Key

See pp. 66–67 for call nos.

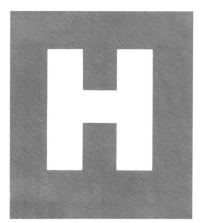

healing

Code Key

health

Hill, Betty and Barney

See pp. 66-67 for call nos.

Hillary, Sir Edmund

Houdini

Code Key

houses

incubus

Code Key

Jesus

Kilner, Dr Walter

See pp. 66-67 for call nos.

King, Katie

Code Key

langur monkey

levitation

see pp. 66–67 for call nos.

ley lines

Lourdes

Code Key

Louviers

magnetism

see pp. 66-67 for call nos.

Magnus, Albertus

Marsh, Othniel Charles

Code Key

Marshall, Mrs Mary

mental illness

mental mediumship

mongoose

Code Key

AA: Alchemy, the Ancient Science

AL: Atlantis and the Lost Lands

CI: The Cosmic Influence

DW: Dream Worlds

EM: Enigmas and Mysteries

GP: Ghosts and Poltergeists

HM: Healing Without Medicine

MB: Minds Without Boundaries

MM: Monsters and Mythic Beasts

see pp. 66–67 for call nos.

music

Nefertiti, Queen

Code Key

Neil-Smith, Reverend J. C.

Nyalmot (Yeti)

See pp. 66-67 for call nos.

Owen, Mrs Julia

Code Key

Pelham, George

pendulum

Piper, Mrs Leonore

Code Key

piper, phantom

pratyahara

See pp. 66-67 for call nos.

precognition

Psychic Self Defense

Code Key

psychic sensitivity

Resurrection, The

Code Key

Resurrection

Ryzl, Dr Milan

Scandinavia

Code Key

AA: Alchemy, the Ancient Science

AL: Atlantis and the Lost Lands

CI: The Cosmic Influence

DW: Dream Worlds

EM: Enigmas and Mysteries

GP: Ghosts and Poltergeists

HM: Healing Without Medicine

MB: Minds Without Boundaries

MM: Monsters and Mythic Beasts

---

scapegoats

sefiroth

self

Shiva

Code Key

see pp. 66-67 for call nos.

Code Key

spiritual body

Stonehenge

Story of Atlantis

Swami Rama

Code Key

Swan on a Black Sea

telepathic interaction

see pp. 66–67 for call nos.

Code Key

Twigg, Mrs Ena

unidentified flying objects (UFOs)

Code Key

union of God and Man

V

Virgin Mary

124

Virgo

werewolves

Code Key

Wesley, Reverend John

witches

Witness Through the Centuries, A

Yukteswar, Sri

Picture Credits